AT TIMES
New and Selected Poems

AT TIMES
New and Selected Poems

BROOKE HORVATH

Seven Stories Press

New York • Oakland • Liverpool

A SEVEN STORIES PRESS FIRST EDITION

Seven Stories Press
140 Watts Street
New York, NY 10013
www.sevenstories.com

Library of Congress Cataloging-in-Publication Data

Names: Horvath, Brooke, author.
Title: At times : new and selected poems / Brooke Horvath.
Description: New York : Seven Stories Press, [2020] | Includes index.
Identifiers: LCCN 2019056444 (print) | LCCN 2019056445 (ebook) | ISBN
    9781609809836 (trade paperback) | ISBN 9781609809843 (ebook)
Subjects: LCGFT: Poetry.
Classification: LCC PS3558.O7274 A8 2020 (print) | LCC PS3558.O7274
    (ebook) | DDC 811/.54--dc23
LC record available at https://lccn.loc.gov/2019056444
LC ebook record available at https://lccn.loc.gov/2019056445

College professors and high school and middle school teachers may order free examination copies of Seven Stories Press titles. To order, visit www.sevensto-ries.com, or send a fax on school letterhead to (212) 226-1411.

Printed in the USA.

9 8 7 6 5 4 3 2 1

ACKNOWLEDGMENTS

Arion: "Stag Hunt."

Free Inquiry: "Hoarding," "Redbud," "Reincarnation," "Still Life with Lamp and Dogs," "'Team Up with Jesus,'" and "The Three Great Ideas of Yacouba Sawadogo."

ISLE: Interdisciplinary Studies in Literature and the Environment: "Notes on a Wren," "Refugium," "Walking the Beach," and twelve sections of "Snapshots of China."

Paterson Literary Review: "Rainouts."

Respect: The Poetry of Detroit Music. Michigan State University Press (2019): "I Thought We'd Never Get Over That First Album."

Sentence: A Journal of Prose Poetics: "Definition." Rpt. *The Prose Poem Project.* 2010. Web; and rpt. *An Introduction to the Prose Poem.* Firewheel Editions (2009).

Sewanee Review: "Courtship in Wartime," "Job's Dream," and "Prejudice."

Snapshots of China. Chapbook. Published by Bunchgrass Press (2015): eleven sections of "Snapshots of China."

So It Goes: "The Driveway" and "I Should Have Been a Painter."

Vocabula Review: "Connect the Dots."

Poems in the first three sections of this book are taken from *In a Neighborhood of Dying Light,* included in the chapbook anthology *Men and Women / Women and Men,* ed. Laura Smith and Larry Smith (Bottom Dog Press, 1994); *Consolation at Ground Zero* (Eastern Washington University Press, 1995); and *The Lecture on Dust* (Bottom Dog Press, 2007).

I wish to thank James McAuley of Eastern Washington University Press and Larry Smith of Bottom Dog Press for their advice and many kindnesses in years past. I also wish to thank the editors of the following periodicals and chapbooks in which many of the poems taken from my previous collections first appeared: *Aethlon: The Journal of Sport Literature, American Literary Review, Antigonish Review, Antioch Review, Apocalypse: Defused or Deferred* (chapbook published by the Poets' League of Greater Cleveland), *Artful Dodge, Boulevard, Calapooya, Cornfield Review, Denver Quarterly, Doggerel, Elysian Fields, Free Inquiry, Great Lakes Review, Greenprints, JAMA: The Journal of the American Medical Association, Jawbone, Key Satch(el), Listening Eye, Lyric, Michigan Quarterly Review, Minneapolis Review of Baseball, Missouri Review, Now in Age I Bud Again* (chapbook published by the Poets' League of Greater Cleveland), *Ohio Poetry Review, Our Voices Heard* (chapbook published by Planned Lifetime Assistance Network of Northeast Ohio and Cleveland State University), *The Plough, Poetry, Poetry in the Parks* (chapbook published by Music in the Air / Columbus, Ohio, Recreation and Parks Department), *The Prose Poem, Sentence: A Journal of Prose Poetics, Sewanee Review, Sparrow, Spitball, Sycamore Review, Tar River Poetry, Texas Review, Tikkun, Unreconciled Passions* (chapbook published by the Poets' League of Greater Cleveland and Spaces Gallery), *Wascana Review.*

At Seven Stories Press, Lauren Hooker treated my sometimes sloppy manuscript with great care and good humor, and Noah Kumin cheerfully pretended that my answers to his questions were helpful.

I am grateful as well to my friend Maura, who gave me good advice for free.

Finally, my sincere thanks to Dan Simon, who knew I was a pain in the ass to work with but was willing to take a chance on these poems because, like David Markson, he believes that "every boy should have a book." I owe Dan many drinks.

CONTENTS

from *In a Neighborhood of Dying Light* (1994)

from *Consolation At Ground Zero* (1995)

from *The Lecture On Dust* (2007)

New Poems

For Ginny—

Comforter and confidante
forgiving conscience
refuge, lover, truest friend

Frank Lima sure was right when he asked, "Why write?
Since the highest enjoyment is a kiss."

"At times . . . I wanted to be a poet."
—HERMANN HESSE

from
In a Neighborhood of Dying Light
(1994)

THE WOMAN IN THE PETER PAN COLLAR

It is 1953, and my mother stands,
in a calf-length woolen skirt,
red cardigan, white cotton blouse,
smiling down at her blue-blanketed
one-month-old. Behind her lies
a stack of lumber piled on dirt
that will stay dirt four years
before becoming grass, and behind that,
a cement-block foundation
above which rises a roughed-in frame,
the house my father, grandfather,
their friends and neighbors
are building for her, for me.

The sun is bright; she squints
toward the camera, trying to smile,
not knowing how long it will take
to raise a house (that once finished
will be too small too soon) or a son,
who once grown will betray
his immigrant roots to run away
and hardly ever write, forgetting
even the names of relations,
yet who will come to waste his time
obsessively fingering Ektachrome clues
to what once was and what,
once once, can never be again.

from IN A NEIGHBORHOOD OF DYING LIGHT

A MATTER OF TREES

Sometimes it's just the sound of words
and their positions on the page, read
with a quiet violence, leaving a stain behind.
As when the weather turned cold
and the black walnuts fell, how
we gathered them, grandfather and I,
our fingers dyed brown and browner,
how one time we entered a field
the theme of which was sheep,
some dead (some dog) some not.
It was upon the dead the accent fell,
the magical horror—a matter of trees
and windy silence like the sound of Ohs
and the odd positioning of bodies,
like the exact word in the right place,
each walnut in its place, its place
the grass, now the basket,
bringing them home for squirrels
to winter on. Buried them mostly,
the squirrels did, as farmers
their sheep—or whatever farmers do
with sheep the dog has ravaged,
leaving their eyes like blank verse,
the dog returning to the field
to scan a line of scarecrow trees.

TRUE ANSWERS TO SINCERE QUESTIONS

The window fan turning
brings in a night
of listless mosquitoes,
lobbed noises, cooling air;
street ball gives way to darkness,
final innings, returning fans.

In the park the sycamores
are hung with locust husks.
Sandwiches have grown funny in their wrappers,
the Nehi a last fizzy swallow of foam.
Ants run across the lazy boy's bare arms;
his girl has grown brown.

The engineer across the street,
home early, uncoils hose
across his burned-out grass,
examines shrubbery,
considers cutting back the hedge,
curses a kick ball in the peas.
He vows never again pole beans,
maybe never again a garden.

In his hot room
the teenager gets ready for a dance
in the popular girl's backyard.
His tight jeans not tight enough,
long hair not long enough,
before the mirror he tries on shirts,
tries not to sweat,
steals album cover stances,
and contemplates himself.

A mother calls her children;
hide and seek is not for her.
Three baths, then quiet for awhile,
a little drink, TV, bed.
Her husband wishes his oak would die,
taking its acorns with it,
leaving garden space.

A radio cheers briefly.
Infrequent couples walk down the ill-lit street.
Someone shoves a wagon off the sidewalk;
it rattles loudly, stops in grass.
Moonlight paws the bushes, climbs the trees.

Factories let out
onto silence.
Cigarettes glow,
then grow apart.
The second shift goes home.

Up the street a car door slams,
bass rumble, soprano giggle.
Upstairs, my wife and daughters sleep
damp beneath cotton sheets,
legs snaking, seeking coolness.

Five minutes in the dark downstairs
behind the latched screen door I stand,
watching, wanting, satisfied.

IN OHIO

I

He walks across his fields
careful of meanings
impressed by thunder
silent in the rain

through tedious tractor afternoons
dreams of bumper harvests
and of drought
of corn-green rows well tended

picking up a clod of dirt
he worries it to soil
listening to the land
speak its leafy language

then cuts a melon tapped for days
before it answered, Ready
waiting, eating, which was better
he couldn't say

II

Dusk, and crickets come alive
cornflowers glow
with fireflies aflirt above them
as fields grow dim

then fog, and nothing
save fog
and through it, crickets
crying for love

closing his eyes
he sees the still corn growing
half-asleep, thinks
I love this as the fish the pond

through the night, crickets
waking, he hears them
until the fog lifts
from morning's fields

FORCING BED

She wants the beans out early
to see them stretch, break earth, and climb—
grumbles at two planned rows of radishes
which neither of us likes
soon they'll clot the ground with white, hot roots
that will crack, spring seed, and rot

but I plant anything that does its growing underground—
potatoes, carrots, turnips, beets—
private, misshapen, dirty
taking time, not
dangling in the air from stake-held strings

       *   *   *

She loves to see creation forming
persuasively in the humid air
swaying, green

I need to know it's happening
in the ground beneath me
fretfully, unseen

WHAT IN THE WORLD WERE
WE THINKING OF?

Today we wore shorts and rugby shirts, sunglasses.
We sat beneath a sycamore on an old quilt
and drank iced tea from Dixie cups.
Our socks and shoes got tossed beside the picnic hamper,
the ball gloves, and the kite
as we risked bees about their business in the clover.
Later, we lay as still as possible,
neither thinking nor talking,
while a killdeer cried out in the blue above us.
A cool breeze blew, but the sun was hot.
We got too much sun, fresh air,
so that now you keep nodding off beside me on the couch
waiting for the late movie to begin,
leftover chicken still uneaten on your plate.

A year from now we won't recall today
any more than other harmless summer days
that passed without any souvenir save sunburn—
days we keep like ticket stubs from summer comedies
that go forgotten in a shirt pocket
until run through the wash and lost.
Photographs of days like these seem pointless,
our early summer legs so white they glow
against the sycamore-shaded green.
When was this? Why did you take this? you'll ask.
What in the world were you thinking of?

Days that leave no urge
to worry them into sense,
no pain worth poetry.
(Who asks why he was happy?

Who bothers to write the answer down?)
Days when sitting in the sun,
the radio tuned to baseball,
was right and necessary,
and intimacy required no confession
of griefs or grudges.
Days when the only sound
was a killdeer's cry or
a ground squirrel's chatter
while we weeded the garden,
our daughters digging in the dirt,
you checking the pepper's progress,
me watching gravity tug
at your breasts as you bent
unmindfully before me.

Today the kite went up without a hitch as high as we had
    string.
I got the camera to work, and you got me to smile.
It was a day when nothing happened
that we will find worth remembering.
If we were mathematical, perhaps we could calculate
the sum of days like these:
lunch on a blanket minus pain equals what?

THE MAN WITH THE AX

The neighbor is angry.
I have chopped down a tree
on our property line.

I loved that tree,
the man next door says,
it was like one of the family.

It was like one of the family,
He said woodenly, I replied,
Laughing and toeing the rotten pulp.

Now, I said, I have a job to do,
and he fell back, locking his door
against the man with the ax.

DOMESTIC VIOLENCE

Senseless beneath the bed sheets,
I lingered into lateness because,
you said, I needed my rest and so,
before it sounded, silenced the alarm.

And so, because I'd overslept,
we began the day with an hour
of high-profile anger, as though
this were part of our morning ritual:

shower, shave, get the coffee going, then fight,
the baby deposited in her high chair
like the pile of clothes I would now
not have time to take to the cleaner's.

Her face grew grave in the face
of our loudness, watching us stir tempests
into our coffee cups, her mouth a rose
closed upon the shrapnel of her stunned silence

as you slammed your way through
the making of toast and scrambled eggs
and I sniped back, cheap shots
about dirty shirts and misdirected kindness

and what alarm clocks are for, the baby
trying to catch my eye with a smile,
the coffee cooling in the pot's dark pool—
as though we had all the time there was,

as though there would always be coffee
in a room with its four walls intact,
as though the baby would always be there
in her chair by the door.

SNAPSHOT WITH FLOWERS

A mother holds her child up
against a floral background,
a Botticelli Madonna, a Capra still,
a young woman simply proud
or proudly shy.
                The camera saw it all,
stole (to reimburse) a little
of their souls, these long-folded
flowers, the mother's smile,
the child's grin.

                They face us bravely,
these two avatars of hubris,
as though they lived before the fall,
and neither to grow old or die.

DETROIT DROPS TWO TO CLEVELAND

For Ralph Stone

The old man sits in his son's garage
his life in boxes behind him
Detroit's humiliation playing to the evening.

He drinks his coffee, listens, forgetting
the score, watching the street, children
lofting balls or cheering runners home.

The radio blares, but the Tigers are fading.
This game is over before it's over.
He can pick it up because his team is on the road.

BRINGING STARS HOME

I

In the dark I rise and walk
beneath stars through snow with whiter stars
a field of light and then a field of light

II

The snowy fields, yes
but, my God, the stars
alone together
and the bare trees,
the drifting night,
the big bang of my breath,
and me walking
away.

III

Without the stars
we stand like Caesar
at Alexandria
great Antony in ruins
Cleopatra dead
the world at our feet
yet empty-handed

IV

This is the myth
explains to me
the path I take
away from you
then back

WEATHERING MARCH

Cancer, when the doctors tell me cancer
like loneliness in old age, its enfeeblement,
like the violence done on any darkened street
when the motor fails, like
nuclear war, when it comes,
will not be unexpected

Unlike this slant of light
through late March woods
across these bare but undead bending branches
glowing maroon and violet-grey and bittersweet

Which is unlooked-for kindness
that takes me back
to fields, to days like these
when I hunted with my dad
when snow hung in the clouds
and no leaves on their stems

Somewhere far between exits
in a clearing barely cleared
from woods caught between the highway
and land readied for corn
a field with its makeshift goals
draws my attention like a crowd

And the air goes supper heavy
raked leaves burn at the ends of drives
and duffled grass
feels soft as sleep
as I dive for a pass

My forty years have leapt
with this light that leaps

like a runner beyond tacklers
fifty more could bring nothing
comforting as this sunshine spiraling down
an easy catch for eager hands

WHY I LIKE BASEBALL

I sometimes feel
I'll return some day
to Concord Avenue
the old house new
the backyard elm still green

Sunny, timeless afternoons
a rubber ball against the garage wall
and back, for hours
or swinging bats, shagging flies
long days of open windows, quiet sounds
that rise and fall like whiffle balls against the blue

Sun, ball, lunch, ball
or aimless walks around the block
past radios tuned to baseball
Sudden Sam on the mound for Cleveland
past sprinklers cutting circles in the grass
intense, wet backyard diamonds

Summer days
no change except occasional rain
the same new game
day after day
the ball
against the wall

from
Consolation at Ground Zero
(1995)

THE SMALLEST COWGIRL ON CLARK STREET

She sits, a ghost child,
astride a broken mule,
yellow now in the photograph,
between her brother Arthur
and sisters Lillian and Esther,
the smallest cowgirl on Clark Street
and the saddest of the children
posed against a lilac bush
in their own front yard
by the traveling photographer
who brought around each summer
this absurd lawn ornament,
this compliant mule, onto which
each child in the neighborhood
was lifted
for the space of an exposure,
just as, later, her son would be
and later still myself
onto a pony, the same look
of glum apprehension mixed
with fantasies of outlaw glory
as though our north Ohio streets
all led to Tombstone or Boot Hill.

The blurred house behind her
in which she lived as a girl
is like the house in which she lived
as a wife on a street
just off Clark Street
where I sit asking myself
the same old questions—
whatever became of Arthur,

of Lillian and Esther? Why
had I never met them?—
shuffling the clues I have
like a pack of photographs
of faces I just can't keep straight,
they look so much alike,
the difference one of background,
of mules or ponies,
of one street or another.

The day she had this picture taken
she sat in a white shift,
black stockings and shoes,
under a Mary Pickford haircut
atop a mild beast
in deference to someone's idea
of the picturesque,
that familial look of gloomy prescience
on her face, as though she
no less than I
knew what was in store for her
once she dismounted—the years
squandered in schools
through which her son
and grandson too would pass,
in rooms and yards in which
she'd play or work
year after year, along streets
whose only change in forty years
would be paving, the shapes of cars,
and the costumes worn by those
who worked or played behind the hedges
walling in each house.
                              The years
of playing someone's wife

until one day she stole away,
stole her son, and moved
for three months into a rented room
six blocks away, not letting her son out
even to go to school, afraid
his father would follow him home
and find her, which eventually
he did.
       The years, years later,
spent curled, corralled, upon a sofa,
smoking and watching television,
never leaving the house, hardly ever
leaving the sofa even to change
the channel, the house running to ruin,
the sofa cushions stuffed with Kleenex
and covered with cigarette burns.

And the years between those years—
before drugs and electroshock
had dragged her back into herself
and everyone pretended not to have seen
the things they saw, before
news of my daughter's birth
caused her to laugh aloud to learn
of one more child saddling up—
when every afternoon
she gathered rocks
from neighbors' driveways,
lugging them home in sacks
like a crazed prospector
and talking to herself, herself
a subject of conversation
in every house down the block
when all the husbands had returned
from work and she returned

to her room to scream
at the photographs
upon her yellowed walls
or to chat quietly
with people on the ceiling
whom only she and I could see.

THE DOLL

When she was little
my sister loved her doll
until the paint flaked
from its sad-luck eyes
and its cloth face, abraded,
bled cotton waste,
until its hair pulled loose
and its body became
a filthy sock, a beaten
stick, dirt with ears.
And she cried, my sister
did, at what love could do.

THE CLOSET

I

The closet rests in a dream of cedar, of clothes
waiting to walk through rooms of blinding sunlight
of which the closet has heard vague rumors.

Although the closet owns a dozen pairs of shoes or more,
like a small child it cannot tie one shoelace,
like a child it longs to run away to sea and change its name.

Wishing to be left alone with its sweaters and golf clubs,
the closet, affectedly signing itself "Clothespress," knows
it has no life of its own, is loved only for its possessions.

In a camphor dialog with darkness, the closet masquerades
    as the space
beneath the bed, the cupboard in which the dead child's
    toys are kept,
knowing itself neither a symbol nor a metaphor.

II

The closet imagines it has sold its memoirs to Hollywood.
Dennis Hopper will star in a David Lynch film
based on the closet's addiction to soiled linen.

Fancying itself a rising star, wishing to be called Cubby,
the closet demands a new wardrobe, better lighting,
covering its walls with pin-ups of guest rooms of the rich
    and famous.

Dreams of success lie piled to the closet's ceiling.
It posts new rules: storage of paint thinner and insecticides
    prohibited!
No clandestine sex during parties! No walking in
    unannounced!

Every week cheap tabloids will lie about the closet's
    contents,
gossip columnists ask "what will the closet hold next?"
The closet will install a pool, be seen in all the right homes.

III

Such adolescent dreams the closet once entertained:
of padded, scented hangers, ample, well-ordered shelves,
tidy rows of pastel frocks with labels reading "Dry Clean
    Only."

Meanwhile, the closet has been forced to take a second job.
Working weekends and evenings as a longshoreman,
the closet begins making off-color remarks about armoires.

The closet feels unfulfilled, seeks excitement in danger,
suggests itself as the perfect place to stash pharmaceuticals.
Here, it whispers, behind the quilts, underneath the mukluks.

Having lost its morals, its sense of right and wrong, the closet
now packs a rod, obscene underwear from mail-order catalogs.
Guests turn away embarrassed from life-size dolls behind
    the tennis dresses.

from CONSOLATION AT GROUND ZERO

IV

The closet cannot sleep, it's so upset. No one
looks any more for his old mitt or her old muff.
No one cares any longer about the secret life of storage
      space.

The closet feigns indifference—its comforting darkness
becomes a refuge in which it fumes and fusses, grumbling
about moths and other things over which it has no control.

Why is there so much dust? the closet queries. How long
      must I entertain
wet umbrellas, boorish boots? Have I lost my youthful vim?
The closet fears it has become a metaphor.

This fear proves stifling. The closet may as well be nailed
      shut,
a locker for bafflement, a cabinet for silence and stale air.
The closet wishes it had never been built.

POSING

A young woman sits on a beach,
her weight on her knees, legs
beneath and behind her,
hands at rest on her thighs.
She is at ease, smiling slightly,
hair wind-blown (the day
appears brisk, whitecaps combing
beneath a storm-thick sky).

She wears a too-large
and therefore charming workshirt
(over a bathing suit, one presumes),
its long sleeves rolled up,
its tails wagging, her expression
one of good-natured indulgence
of the photographer who has placed her
in this *U.S. Camera* pose.

She starred in plays in high school
and will soon be offered a screen test
by Universal, but by then
she will have married the photographer
and become pregnant and will say,
with the photographer's complete endorsement,
that mothers don't leave their children
to become movie actresses.

So she will perform instead in the kitchen,
before the washer, at little theaters,
will give readings to women's clubs
and church groups. Local papers
will praise her, and old women

will call her dear and clap their bony hands.
But this will not suffice. And whether
the photographer regrets her decision,
I do not know. But I know I do,
and am sorry.

ABRASION

Grandfather hammers risers. They are both
perfectly fit.
          At the business end
of his intensity, teeth clench
upon a mouthful of finishing nails
and the dark, chewed mess
of a cigar stub, eyes bright
with expertise and grandfatherhood.

We are two and I am two and beside him,
eyes closed against the pounding,
small arm raised authoritatively
in a gesture of command.
He always liked to tell
how I helped him build that house
through all those long, nuisance hours,
evenings and Saturdays,
how I never left his side, learned
the names of tools—
rip saw, caulking gun, putty knife,
sander, rasp, Phillips head—
holding, handing them to him,
steadying the boards he sawed,
sawdust on both our knees.

Now, thirty-three years later,
it is my fate, and his, to direct him
once again, something like sawdust
obscuring his finish.
          And I think
how age and illness have left us
without the tools we need,
have rubbed me softly raw.

THE WEED PULLER

Feet bare, kneeling
hands dirt-covered
fingers rooting among seedlings
he bows, rises, bows again
rises, forehead sweat
falling to earth, greenness
running through his brain
like water through a hose

If he could spare the weeds
not desire ripened
corn, pale yellow-white
and sweet, this moment would last—

CHRISTMAS EVE

In the photograph, relatives have gathered
who gather now for funerals only.
But here they sit to share stories and food,
watching their children wrestle the wrapping
from small gifts.
           My grandfather, now adrift
in time, face haloed in cigar smoke,
glasses giving back the flashbulb's glare,
sits smiling at his brother Joe, now dead,
beside his younger brother Bill (now dead),
who sits, debonair, legs crossed,
behind a thick Hungarian mustache
in a dark suit and painted tie,
cigarette poised in portrait pose.
Bill sits beside my mother,
caught off-guard beside an empty chair
(the photographer's) and very clearly tired
of this endless round of ritual visits,
her head resting on a braceleted arm, eyes shut.

And I am on her lap and am two,
face obscured by a package too big for me
and which grandfather will soon help open
with a pocketknife.
           Everyone (save me)
holds drinks—Haller's SRS neat
or ginger ale festooned with maraschino cherries,
hi-balls for the older kids.
About us, paper and presents lie thinly strewn,
for gifts were fewer and more modest then
though there were more of us.

                    The furniture,
like the clothing, is of another place
and time, unredeemable, long before Santa
gave way to Scotch and water, expensive gifts,
and funerals, when sentiment was unnecessary
and the trees held fragile blown balls,
frayed cords of painted lights, and paper chains
lengthening year by year.
                    Long ago,
when Christmas was an endless round of visitations
we thought would never end.

MOTHER AND CHILD REUNION

Sandalled toes
arching toward the ground,
legs out straight before her
like a bird alighting,
then levered behind her
with a modest shift of weight,
she swings with her child
on her lap, one hand
secure about a chain,
the other about her child,
the chain caught
in the bend of her arm.
Together they cleave the humid air,
creating their own weather,
which blows their hair
about their faces,
and then away,
trailing a wake of laughter
through which momently
they plunge.

The child grins beneath
his mother's smile,
one small hand tight
about the chain,
swinging in a lazy arc
that carries them back
and forth
past the empty seat
beside them,
above the heads
of zinnias and morning

glories in a garden
gone to ruin
in someone's long ago
backyard in a year
we might deduce.

Whose garage, whose yard,
whose vacant seat
we do not know.
All that can be said is
that it is summer
in a world almost lost to us
wherein a mother and her child
swing as they have always swung
midway between two points
in space and time
(enjoying, if they only knew it,
the greater luxury not of having
but of being memories),
a world of modest pleasures,
freshly cut zinnias,
the rocking of a child,
affection that can hold each other
closely in the vanishing day
of swinging summer
with a grip both casual
and sure.

It is a snapshot buried
in the mind's dim locker
of two lives that should have worked
and largely did, and to which
I cannot not return.
For I want to hug this child to me,

holding him easily,
to give his mother a few hours
to herself, a chance
to weed this garden or
to swing the car in that garage
out into the street and off,
perhaps to have her hair redone.
I'd like to ask her how she'd like
a heart-shaped box of chocolates
some Valentine's Day,
or dimestore earrings
for her birthday, or maybe
a bouquet of daffodils
picked by small hands
from a neighbor's flowerbed;
would like to tell her
of the hours she will pass
seeking cherries and sweet corn
at roadside stands,
just passing time,
or pulling a wagon endlessly
around the block
to lull this child into slumber.

And I would like to tell this boy
that Little League is supposed
to be fun, that his swimming teacher
will not let him drown,
that one day a girl no older than he
will call him on the phone—
and he should not hang up embarrassed.
I'd promise that one Halloween
he'll be a pirate, and the next
a cowboy with a real lasso

and cowhide chaps. I think
I could explain fractions
so he'd understand, and I'd hint
that it will not be necessary
to worry so about everything
from grades to Vietnam,
that he'll survive his every world
at least until he is as old as I.

Of course they both
survived this world
through which they seem to move
so effortlessly.
And if, along the way,
they lost the cowboy hat,
the pirate mask, the dimestore
earrings, and the daffodil
pressed into a book of plays,
these were not to be
their largest loss,
which was the love
not for each other
(that they kept)
but for this too-small child,
this too-young mother
left dangling on a swing
somewhere in someone's
long-ago backyard
in a year we could deduce.
Love left behind
like pools of shadow
in their laps or, rather,
mislaid somewhere
like a heart-shaped Valentine

amid a wealth
of sun-struck days
through which
they continue swinging,
their large
and rust-stained hands
clenching fatigued chains
connected to an empty seat.

FOR PAUL PACK, MANAGER OF THE LITTLE LEAGUE EAST OHIO VENDING TEAM

My mother said he was a quiet man, meaning a nice man,
but the kid who never got to play said
his father said our manager was a lush.
And he works for an exterminator, the kid said—
he's a drunk fuckin' bug-killing loser.

When he loaded our gear into his dirt-on-rust Biscayne
and pulled away in his Ohio Vending cap, trailing smoke,
he looked like a loser no matter how we'd done.
The kid's father said so, who was some big-shot executive,
which is why his son, the kid said, never got to play.

So whenever he yelled at me for turning my head on a
        grounder
or for backing off Bob Maxwell's fastball,
I'd tell myself so what? He's just a loser—something
most of us were only on the field and only sometimes
and almost always because of someone else.

And if he was a loser, that helped explain our defeats,
and so what then if maybe he knew that off the field
is where we did our hiding behind a ball cap,
and so what if on the field, like him, we thought we had a
        chance
mostly if others managed to fail more than we did?

After one game when I'd refused to try to bunt
he chewed me out in front of everyone, yelled
about teamwork and how I wasn't his only shortstop.
He benched Frankie Fields for a week once for talking dirty,
shook his head and lit a Lucky when parents booed.

One time he pulled the team and forfeited the game
after Don Hawk hit a homer but got called out
for failing to touch third, then bought us all Nehi's
and said how, yes, small things matter
but were no reason to take a home run away from a boy.

When he gripped my wrists to show me how to hit to right,
I thought he'd break my arms, but I've him, I think,
to thank for making the all-star team,
and so what if his sweaty tee-shirt smelled like Raid,
and so what if one time at practice,

watching the kid who never got to play run out a lucky
        grounder,
he joked to his coach, our mailman, that some day
they'd have to get a calendar and time the kid,
the coach grinning in a way that left me certain
mailmen were callused and cruel and in love with danger.

Off the field, having given what light he had
until the next game or weekend practice,
when the Biscayne, its muffler dragging,
pulled into Gibby's down the street from the ball field
and across from General Industries, where the big shot worked,

he became for us as meaningless as the sunsets that only
        called us home,
as pure of meaning as the game itself until upon its
        blankness
we wrote ourselves with every error and awkward catch
who were ourselves like the sheets of exterminator
        stationery
on which before each game that drunk wrote down our
        sunny names.

THE COLOR OF THE IRIS

My poems come like angels' visits
—few and far between, leaving my head
aching like a first frost.

But this could hardly interest you,
who sleep like a bulb beneath warming soil,
an iris of complex awakening.

                          Your face
is a room in early April, skirted
furniture and crewel embroidery, & behind your eyes
the knick-knacks children love to ogle
when they visit an aging aunt
always just returning from her travels.

Yesterday in the car we drove fast and sang,
the green world grew white and windblown
& I told you how I used to want love to come
—like snowflakes falling,
the kind children make in grade school
from folded paper,
no two alike, and no more than two
intact.
        Now it seems better
as a field of knee-deep snow beyond the window,
the children cutting silhouettes
for their classroom wall
or bundling up in overcoats
to flap their arms in their own backyards.

Meanwhile, the floor remains covered
with clipped snippets of paper
which the children leave
everywhere they've been.

And as I knew they would,
blue shadows fill the corners of your face.
They are the color of the iris just before its petals fall.
Or have it your way—they are like snow angels' wings.

But for now, or at least until later,
let's get something straight.
Put your hand on the Oldsmobile's hood
and tell me: who's been driving this car?
How did it get so muddy?
& how did these flowers get caught in the grille?

"BAG OF LIFE #38"

is what she bends to write across
the bottom of the monotype, each word
as small as someone else's loss,
as faint as something overheard.

The thirty-seven prints that rest
beside her in a numbered stack
are as alike as hand and press
allow: against a smear of black

a blur of white, a bag, that holds
some mystery left unexplained
by what we're shown and what we're told.
We wouldn't know what the bag contained

except that it's there before her where
she sits amid her work, a dull
enigma spoken like a prayer
to paper and the press's pull,

then emptied and refilled. A box
of bric-a-brac is also near
at hand: post cards, a doll that talks,
some ticket stubs, two porcelain deer,

pink shells, brown leaves, a book of poems,
a clutch of bundled letters, a scrap
of calico. From such stuff stems
the life she shelters in her lap

before it's placed into the sack.
Then, after one more cigarette

is shaken from her crumpled pack,
the plate is cleaned and inked for yet

a thirty-ninth impression whose
distinction resides alone in what
cannot be seen by us who choose
to find the artist in a rut

and, joking, ask, where is the bag?
where is the life? and ask her why
what's inside matters, what's the gag,
and what does all this signify?

We look and judge the work misnamed,
unwilling to see the dark's her home
in which a life's been kept, reclaimed
from the monotonous and monochrome.

ACCADEMIA: FLORENCE

A man reaches out to touch, flesh to stone,
a Michelangelo statue.
It is not the famous Carraran David,
towering above tourists, aloof,
polished giant toward which
their cameras, guidebooks, fingers point.

The man is no paparazzo.
He holds no camera, has left his guidebook
on a bench somewhere down the hall.
Perhaps someone will take it, or
he'll forget it. No matter.
It tells him nothing of the sculptor's
need, or his, for contact with another;
of how, once caught,
he couldn't let go, by finishing free
his half-formed brother,
however cold or captive he might be—
perhaps because, cold and captive and half-formed,
he needed a hand still
upon his chisel-scarred flank.

The man reaches out, although
someone is doubtless watching
to see that such things don't happen.
As the figure struggles
in his marble prison, so the man
struggles against the crowd,
his fear of seeming foolish,
his reticence, forgetting
how many lire equal bed and breakfast,
how far he's come to stroke a stone.

With his hand upon
a shoulder upon which
Michelangelo once rested,
this man, too, just now, stands caught,
half in, half out of bondage.

PIAZZA SAN MARCO: VENICE

I wish I could have been the one
to take her order,
to deliver on a silver tray the iced coffee
she now stirs with a slow spoon,
though I would settle for being the cold April wind
across the Piazza San Marco
that turns her jacket collar up
and fans her hair about her face.
She doesn't mind, notices the wind
less than she does the waiter,
no more than her downcast eyes
observe the tourists, pigeons, louring sky.

No one else sits outdoors today
before the storied Florian,
whose Martini chairs and tables drift
in a stone sea behind her
with the ghosts of Byron and Henry James
(who would, I think, enjoy her,
each, of course, in his own way).

A copy of the *Herald Tribune* lies folded
in the chair beside her.
Perhaps she follows a ball club
somewhere in the American Midwest,
or owns stock, or has a concern for Aldo Moro.
Possibly she desires only
the shape of her own words,
the voices they recall.

She sips her coffee,
thumbs a Michelin Green Guide

I would give anything to be
for the chance to describe for her
Titian madonnas and old monasteries,
to direct her through the twisted streets
that all lead to where she sits,
to tell her stories of the Bridge of Sighs
(though again, I'd willingly settle
for being her glass of iced coffee,
or her wind-tossed jacket, or that long, dark hair
seeking the attention of her downcast eyes).

WILD POPPIES

Jeu de Paume, Paris

A woman moves easily through a field of poppies,
casually holding a gentian-blue parasol. She looks
lost in thought, seems to feel herself alone,
although her daughter, almost hidden
by the waist-high grass, follows closely after,
clutching confidently before her a bouquet
red as the ribbon around her hat, her dress
trailing cerulean dabs behind her,
as though her passing caused cornflowers,
morning glories to open bluely.
Indeed, they both seem as alone as you,
just to the right of a starry Van Gogh night,
despite each other, despite a second woman
and child farther back up the hill, who stand
watching them (or would, had they eyes
in the brushstroke faces).

You and I that day, as I recall, were all eyes
intent on color, what particular shades could mean
and feel like. Outside, in the shops,
in the public gardens, other flowers bloomed,
other women moved easily among them,
and for a while you had been one of them,
luminous in a white skirt and muslin blouse
through which your breasts shone darkly.

That night, at the Hotel Paris-Nice,
your skirt and blouse blazed across
the darkness of our room like falling stars,
and a cool field opened before us

in which our blanched faces hung
like gardenias, which stain when touched.
Through our open window came the sound,
parasol cool, of someone playing the blues
down in a café, her words folding,
bending, falling like petals
from a fistful of flowers I was once caught,
as in a painting, passionately holding.

COOK'S TOUR: ROME

I have pictures here of things I don't remember seeing,
places I don't remember being, in "Rome, the Eternal—
Treasurehouse of Western Culture," as Fodor's has it.
I do recall a bag of artichoke sandwiches eaten in the rain
on the steps of the Temple of Venus and Rome,
you coming down with bronchitis and having to spend four
    days
coughing in bed, how I waited out a rain delay in a café
along the Via Veneto getting wired on two
or three too many espressos and reading P.G. Wodehouse.
And, of course, the Colosseum, where we walked the day
we arrived, talking of Daisy Miller, where a cabbie
too insistent, too persuasive to ignore, accosted us.
For 20,000 lire, give or take a thousand, he said
he'd show us Rome, and did he ever. Gothic charges
across well-defended intersections and persecutions
of the slow and indecisive brought us down Via Appia Antica
to the catacombs of San Callisto, where this madman
bullied us to the front of a line of tourists,
you remarking how the best way out is through,
me counting lire and thinking how sweetness draws flies.
Then on past ruins coming thick as flies—the Forum,
the Temple of the Vestal Virgins, the Arch of Janus,
Nero's House of Gold, the Baths of Diocletian—
to a screeching halt in heavy traffic, where our driver
made you stand in the middle of the street
before Hadrian's pyramid and ordered me to take your
    picture
because "this is really something." We ran
to the Protestant cemetery to see the graves
of Keats and Shelley, our cabbie bewildered
(just two more stiffs, I'm sure he thought impatiently).

Back in the cab, we barreled past the Pantheon,
the Villa Borghese, Victor Emmanuel's ugly monument,
the mandatory fountains and markets so beloved
by us Americans (the Fountain of Trevi shut down and dry).
We stopped at San Pietro in Vincoli where a priest
charged us 500 lire each (and made us leave five minutes later)
to see Michelangelo's Moses and the chains that bound St.
    Peter
("my baby's got me locked up in chains," the Beatles sang
in my foolish head the while). Last stop, San Paolo fuori le
    Mura
where again photography was urged upon us, this time the
    two of us
posed before a statue of St. Paul, apostle to us gentiles,
sword in hand, scowling out at a taxing, godless world.

And here, I thought, is the scam unfolded, us smiling
like two American Express chumps about to have our
    wallets lifted,
our guide running back toward his cab, my camera in hand,
surely to jump in and off. But no. He turned, fiddled,
cursed two nuns who dared to walk into the viewfinder's field,
squinted, and snapped our picture, the only one we have
of both of us together, light bouncing off the church's gilt
    façade
like a nimbus about St. Paul and us (you and I smiling
apprehensively, to be sure), the shot well framed and focused,
the exposure exact: a fragment saved from all those ruins,
for which I must offer a late apology and thanks.

TOMORROW WE DISCUSS COTTONWOODS

My father-in-law catches me reading again.
Seeing I am not doing anything important,
he begins to explain how dandelions go to seed
and how the wind blows the seed every which way
depending on which way the wind is blowing.
He tells me if I want to know what it is like to be busy,
I should try to keep a yard free of dandelions
when all the neighbors' yards are only dandelion patches.

He thinks I do not know such things
(last week he told me how a lawnmower works).
He thinks I read hopelessly book after book
in search of the true story of dandelions,
how they go to seed that the wind blows every which way.
Interrupting me, he is only being kind, only saving me time.

EVANGELIST WITH CHILD

Her face is plain
but her eyes are lovely,
blue as the Word is true,
her boy well-scrubbed,
bow-tied, tongue-tied.

I watch her watching me
as she says they've come
to save me. From sin
(of course) and out of love.
Now, can they have a minute

of my time to prove it?
To prove what? The sin
part or the love part?
I could, I think, scare them away
by staring at her breasts.

I think they've come perhaps
to save themselves, me
just another trading stamp
to be redeemed when
their book is full.

But "out of love" is
what she said, and she
looks it, though she
doesn't seem to care and anyway
is full of beautiful words

like the book she opens,
like those the boy, on cue,

recites. And anyway
her eyes are beautiful.
And anyway, who am I to judge

who's admitted his depravity?
But even so, how could I
toss scorn over this boy's head
and into some boy's mother's
strained, plain face?

A MARY HAGGADOT

1. The Annunciation

It is said lilies nodded at the window,
from a vase on the vanity where she sat
admiring herself, her sky-blue eyes
and the high cheekbones her father praises
framed in the wimple of mother's shawl.

Her mouth red from mother's lipstick,
she had been playing dress-up,
having grown too old for her closetful
of dolls and board games and paints,
the picture books and puzzles.

Tired of make-believe, she wants to ask
if the boy next door can come for lunch
and wonders uneasily about all these lilies
sprouting, it seems, everywhere,
even between the tiles of her bedroom floor,

when suddenly a knock at the door
shakes the sign she's posted there
(Private! Keep Out! This Means You!),
announcing the arrival of a stranger
lovely as the new girl at school.

He holds—what else?—a lily, kneels,
bows his head politely (though his eyes
never leave hers), then begins to speak
(it is like music) of things mother said
they would discuss when she is older.

Outside, where her swingset rusts,
the rain that beat the flowers down all morning
has stopped. Suddenly the yard
is filled with doves, and the grass has grown
very green, the sky very blue.

2. Adoration of the Shepherds

You'd think they'd never seen a baby
or a woman before, blushing as they are,
the sweet, bumpkin things they say,
as though her child were a lamb.

Watching him sleep, she wonders
all the usual things, what his first
words, say, will be. It is said
hers were "O Deus, ego amo te"!

She'd forgotten that family story
until the stranger who called
nine months ago reminded her,
but how did he know the things he knew?

He'd told her then about the cattle lowing
in the dead of night, the shepherds,
the lilies out of season, the name
they'd choose—and it all has been just so.

He said he was the angel Gabriel, but all
she knows is that he had about him that day
the oddest glow, and when he appeared
there was suddenly from somewhere music.

The shepherd boys who've made her room

their own have grown sleepy, and she too
is nodding off. She looks to put out
the light, the softest, warmest light

she's ever seen. It seems to spill
from the cradle, from somewhere just
above her head, from the chair where Joseph
snores in the otherwise darkened room.

Shadows move like blue doves in the rafters,
and every mundane object in this light
is beautiful, as though the world
had fallen for once in love with itself.

3. Madonna of the Paintings

She thinks she's looking good again,
the way she looked when she was single,
her face in the window's mirror
a portrait by Botticelli or Richard Avedon,
though this has, she suspects,
something to do with the odd light
now constantly gathering about her,
its intense, painterly quality.

However that may be, it is true
someone is always falling by to ask
over the ceaseless hammering
from the garage (where Joseph turns
all his nervous energy into chairs
and vanities) if he might "do her."
Usually she acquiesces though already
the walls are plastered with their efforts.

Like the carved and chiseled likenesses
filling the basement, the paintings all look
much the same to her, their titles silly
and unimaginative—*Madonna of the Goldfinch,*
Madonna of the Fish, Madonna with Angels.
There must be three dozen called *Madonna and Child.*
(She put a stop to that—all that sitting around
was not good for a small boy).

Now she sends Jesus down to the store,
or out to help his father plane and varnish,
whenever some Italian or German-speaking genius
arrives with his brushes and apprentices
to pose her "just so" in her favorite chair
and slave until they lose the light,
then spends the evening drinking wine
with Joseph and talking frames.

Studying the paintings, she supposes Joseph
responsible for some of the details—
the star, the more-or-less accurate description
of that flea-bag motel, those useless gifts
of frankincense and myrrh. But who, she wonders,
told these guys about the lilies, the angel,
or the way the sky that day
turned such a funny shade of blue?

4. Landscape with Saint John

He is a filthy little man
with eyes like Charlie
Manson's, but he has a halo
just like hers (a nuisance
she's grown used to long ago)—

she can see it glowing
as he wades into the water,
away from the small crowd
whose neglected cattle low
on the darkening hillside.

What John's up to she can't guess,
nor that angel—the same one
again—who's just arrived
to hold her son's red blazer importantly
while he follows after John,
just as the setting sun
turns every tree into a cross
and the water—where several men
sit fishing and a woman
washes clothes—into blood.

As she turns for home
where she should be busy
fixing supper, she notices
John's halo floats
above his head like a platter
and that in the distance
beyond the farm-cluttered
hills and evening chores
the sky has turned again
that otherworldly blue.

5. The Crucifixion

She tosses, groans,
the pillow damp,
her legs snaking
beneath the twisted,

immaculately white
sheets of the safe
bed, of lightning
whiplashing across
the sky, lost
in an hallucination
of soldiers
and sinister locals,
cowed friends
and bodiless,
gawking angels,
the pale sun lost
to abrupt dark,
all color draining
from the world.

His resignation,
his bravado and
inhuman
forgiveness
washing over
the crowd,
she shrinks
from the storm's
eye, turns
in the tangled
sheets, her face
frozen
in disbelief,
by her belief
from deep within
this nightmare
that having allowed
such a thing

to happen
has been, if it
was anything,
to sin,
by her suddenly
knowing why
the sky was always,
like her eyes,
that terrible shade
of blue.

Caught in the absolute
black of sleep
between one sun
and another,
she moans,
the nightmare
inescapable,
the final scene—
her son now
in her arms, his
splintered body,
her bloody dress—
frozen, time
falling away
like a camera
pulling back,
leaving them
a tableau
of defeat
in the provinces,
the birthdays,
the supper-time
laughter, a child's

small cries
in the night
lost in events
that cannot
contain them,
both of them
inhuman now, dim
as a painting
needing restoration,
the sky giving way
to blank stretches
of canvas, her sorrow
fading to grey,
the paint
flaking bluely
even from her eyes.

6. *Jesus Appearing to His Mother*

She always had to laugh whenever
Anne and the others reminisced.
Jesus was in fact such a bad boy—

like the day the neighborhood kids
made fun of him and he got the bushes
behind the ball field to beat them into tears

(later, Joseph had to do the same,
paddling the boy's small bottom
with his halo until it almost broke)

or the times they caught him showing off,
asking in church impossible questions
or pretending to raise the dead.

But this last trick was anything
but funny, appearing to her where she sat
exhausted after months without a word,

her letters all returned "addressee unknown,"
the days of gossip and insinuation,
and these last nights of nothing but bad dreams—

her son arrested in the dead of night, whipped
and mocked, tried and executed, his friends
avoiding her, and the one found hanged.

Then there he stood, smelling of the grave,
in his feet and hands bloody holes, his side
split open, his face scratched and bleeding.

But more mysterious was what he said
as he turned to leave with that angel waiting
in the failing blue of evening. "Fear not,"

he whispered, "I've come so that you'd know
that everything I did and said was true
was true."

7. Death of the Virgin

She lies drowning in the pool
of her gown, surrounded
by so many haloed men
the room's brightness
hurts her eyes.

She regrets, too late of course,
neglecting the other children,
but the entire business

was so confusing and Joseph
so constantly bewildered,
his saws and hammers his only comfort.

Thinking about such things,
thinking against the soporific
she's been given,
she cannot shake the feeling
she is no one's mother
and everyone's, her son's wife,
two fathers' daughter,
and ghostly if here at all.

She would like to talk
about this bafflement
that makes her forget
what she wants to remember—
her son's first step,
first tooth, first word—
but Anne (*Saint* Anne now,
like everybody else she knows)
is dead and these old men
so somber, thumbing even now
their small, thick books
and staring heavenward.

They don't, she thinks, see
a thing, don't have a clue.
For them, it's all make-believe,
the sort of thing the magi do
every weekend at the Rivoli.

She studies her hands
afloat on the gown's cool surface,
the same hands

that washed out diapers,
rubbed her round belly,
and felt the beauty once
of her own cheekbones
as she sat self-raptured
before the bedroom mirror.

Above her and this crowd
of Dutch uncles
she thinks she sees
that superior angel again,
Gabriel, she believes
he said his name was
(there have been so many,
really, who've called).
He is getting to be a nuisance
worse than any halo.

He looks years older,
but she notices
he still has his damned lily—
this time pinned to his lapel—
and that he's brought his friends along—
Michael, Uriel, Raphael,
and those three
who never said their names.

It must be the medicine,
because they look as though
they are parting clouds
where the raftered ceiling
used to be,
revealing someone
who looks, she thinks,
(or so it is said)

like her first husband.
He is holding their son
and gazing sadly down
into her sky-blue eyes
as though upon a world
that until now he thought
he had only imagined,
and in which he had never
quite believed.

MY GIRL

for Susan

On that predawn Tuesday
no birds sang, & I
couldn't find my way home
down these shuttered,
unfamiliar streets.
I thought how strange
the passing cruiser
did not stop me, but
went on, business as usual,
as though the police
didn't know a felon
when they saw one.
I thought how circumspect
the girl who served me coffee,
how well she carried on
as though nothing were wrong.

Beyond the window
birds flew about like
the uninformed while I
tried to dial a number,
tried not to think
of the doctor, how
he took me aside
to toss the word
"Down's" at me like
a poisoned crumb,
dispassionately, like
slapping on the cuffs,
like asking a simple
question: do you take
cream in your coffee?

from CONSOLATION AT GROUND ZERO

(Did I? I
couldn't remember.)

As the coffee cooled
I thought how I
had thought first
of myself, my face
counterfeiting masculinity,
my eyes holding back
their tears. How my heart
fluttered & took flight.
How I thought then
of your mother, exhausted
down the hall,
where your cries,
had you cried,
could not reach her.
How only then I thought
of you, small bird,
unmoving in your nest.

While the long worm
Of an IV fed you, I stood
quietly beside you,
watching other fathers
above their daughters cooing,
thinking how you & I
had somehow failed
to reach our destination.
& as your small breast
barely rose and fell,
I looked for traces
of the crime where
your smile should
have been, though you
were lovely as autumn,
and delicate as down.

IN THE NEO-NATAL INTENSIVE-CARE UNIT

We are children here, hesitant
to speak or touch, afraid of reprimand.
The nurses, doctors are adult; they tell us
to wash our hands, to be careful; they
say that everything will be all right;
they remind us when it's time for bed, where
dreams fill with stopped monitors and alarms,
intravenous tubing, and disembodied cries like clues
dropping amid the tears and gauze
through which your eyes, Susan, stare
blindly, your dry mouth working soundlessly.

Susan, if I could, I would hurt instead
with a clean, hard, physical pain, would take
this needle into my larger, drying vein
and have my stomach aspirated, which finds,
like yours, nothing but itself to work upon.
I would breathe through your congested lungs,
escaping this nauseous sickness of heart
that draws me back to stroke your red and jaundiced head
so new it shows the shape of birth, the stain
and strain of passage, to lift and hold your tiny hand
that does not feel or know me, though you hold
my life unstably as your own, as I would
hold yours, though tightly, tightly,
though not so tight you'd bruise or break.

THREE DEAD BIRDS

Birds, my daughter says, pointing.
Eyes, mouth, feet—
touching after each word
herself.

Baby birds, I say,
as though baby birds
always lay
in a broken sprawl on the sidewalk,
as though Watts was always burning,
as though death were a lesson in diction.

THE *ENCYCLOPÆDIA BRITANNICA* USES DOWN SYNDROME TO DEFINE "MONSTER"

humani nil a me alienum puto.
—Terence

I

The encyclopedia's definition leaves my daughter holding hands with Grendel, the Cyclops, Frankenstein's monster, the mythic deformities of hell.

Chancing upon this definition leave me face to face with the unspeakable.

II

She is a monster who cries, recites with her sister the alphabet, has fallen in love with the boy at preschool who opens her yogurt for her.

She is a monster who meets with fear and stares outside and inside holds the usual human emotions imprisoned by more than usual inarticulateness.

III

My insurance company will not pay for her therapy. Therapy, a letter tells me, is covered only following an accident.

My insurance company does not believe in genetic accidents. My insurance company covers only human beings.

IV

The *Encyclopædia Brittanica,* with its assurance that truth is tidy and knowable and human-sized, can shove its learning up its human ass.

It is anything human that is alien to me.

V

My monster's favorite shirt has four hearts across its front. I ask her why she likes this shirt so much, and she points to the hearts.

You like hearts, I ask. But she shakes her head no, pointing again to each heart in turn and saying carefully: mommy, daddy, sister, me.

ARKANSAS FUNERAL 1986

As the cortege turned down another road to nowhere,
rolled with the cotton lint across fields like open ovens,
the six pall-bearers wadded into the dusty Buick Skylark
bitched about the local niggers, who after all these years
were still insisting on integrated schools.
                                        Or rather,
four bitched and one defended: give them, he said,
a job pays enough so they can afford a house,
they'll take care of that house almost as good
as we would. "We" meaning them,
these five friends and near relations
of the dead man, not one of them under sixty.

"We" did not mean me, a stranger dragooned
when, at the last minute, the sixth pall-bearer
failed to show. Not that six were required.
The old man even in his walnut box weighed little more
than a couple sacks of cotton, was now
what he always said he felt when ill: puny.
I was a fifth wheel, a silent partner,
one of those unnecessary people put up with
because even the dead have their needs:
a serge suit, revival hymns and scripture
in God's well-kept house, relatives teary-eyed
and sweaty from a night in Arkansas motels,
a full contingent of men to lift and tote.

So with the casualness of seeking a fourth for bridge
or hiring someone to help in the fields,
I was asked to lend a hand, who was what to the dead man?
The long-haired northerner who'd carpet-bagged his way

into the old man's granddaughter's bed,
who pronounced "Cairo" as though it were a city in Egypt
and forked through his greens as though he thought
his food was somewhere underneath.

As we made our way to where the car would finally stop
and we'd spill from its hot insides like cotton from a boll
to leave the old man in the ground he loved,
talk turned to other out-of-favor neighbors,
to why the Amish were such shits.
                              No, I said,
if they won't wear buttons, they're German Baptists.
They're German Baptists, I said,
while in the roadside fields our passing dusted,
where men, black and white, bent hoeing cotton,
each, as he saw us coming,
laid down his hoe, took off his hat,
and stood at attention as we passed.

ALOPECIA AREATA

1. No Other God Before Me

My daughter touches the spot
where her hair used to be.
The spot is spreading like a stain
across her blond beauty.

She does not know why
she touches the spot, except
that we do, doctors do.
She does not know
she is growing again different
from other children,
she who with her Down's
and leaky heart
already had the makings
for a mess of grief.
She does not know why
I come to sit beside her bed,
holding her hand,
an impotent barricade
between her
and a molesting god.

She touches
her ointment-smeared baldness
and smiles,
seeking my approval,
or as though reminding me
that the ones we love
are loved not despite
but for their flaws
because so much of what we are
is the result of them.

I would like to believe that.
I would like to believe
many things.
I wipe the ointment
from her fingers,
and she smiles again,
her eyes looking deep
into the heaven of mine.

2. Sins of the Father

I find your hair
in your sister's fist,
on the blanket,
in a weave above
the bathtub drain
like signs to somewhere
no one wants to be
or traces of a plundered
mine or clues
to an unsolvable
crime which somehow,
sometime I committed,
some sin for which you
must atone, your condition
the result of mine.

Every time you touch
your head or bring it
too near the baby's
capricious grasp
we wince. We flirt
with loss in the most
innocent acts,
washing your hair,
tying it back.

Each time I brush
the tangles from
your ponytail,
I grow more intimate
with the god of Moses.

3. Every Hair Is Numbered

Before we set out
on this path that is ours
I anoint your head
until its bald scalp flames,
I who am still the ark
of what will one day be
your memories, you
whom I know more intimately
than I know myself,
having counted
each step taken,
each nose bleed
and lifted spoon,
every hair that falls.

As we walk along,
I count each hair left
with each step taken
and tell myself
no one will love you now
for the wrong reasons.
Nearer our destination,
I imagine hands suddenly
reaching out, so small
they lose themselves in mine,
                              so large
mine pour into them
like darkness.

OCTOBER FROST

Last night's frost
has hung the pepper plants
with black and cost
the zinnias all their color.

Beside the gate
among dry summer weeds
half-dead spiders wait
for colder weather.

Time to gather
marigold heads,
to tie together
ice-tight lengths of twine.

Tubers underground
may linger, but almost all
the green has browned,
stands tangled as balled twine.

Stiff hose, wire fence
must be rolled up, stakes
pulled and scraped. Now diligence
is done. One waits for winter.

The rush to use the harvest
is passed; the daily watch
over change, relieved. Unrest
among the rows falls silent.

The peace that passed
when spring began descends
upon the garden. The massed
life gone, the cold ground mends.

DECEMBER TULIPS

I thought tulips
were coming up through the December ground.
What they were, I don't know,
perhaps misguided tulips.

And so, like someone
Underground or windowless,
unable to judge the light left,
to see rain strike morning's shadows,

I forgot the season,
the date, the clouds
that promised an end
to matted leaves, muddy fields.

On a reprehensible street
of porches chaired by tattered sofas,
hedges full of bottles,
as the day shivered,

I found myself
in momentary April
walking oddly
beneath a kited sky.

No one was near to set me straight,
so I walked on, expecting warm rain
and pollen breezes, while broken bits of Christmas
blazed up like Easter.

HELLO

My father built the house
we lived in, held down
a job he didn't like,
and went to college
thirteen years, nights,
to earn a better one.
Seen from a distance
with book or T-square
or trowel in hand he seemed
to overflow with know-how.

My mother pulled me
in a wagon around
and around the block
or drove me into the country
for cherries or sweet corn
weekend after weekend
after weekend
so dad could study or shellac
in peace. When he was home,
the watchwords were
"be quiet" and "don't."
There was no password
save as I grew older
the boxed game mother and I
whisperingly played
at the kitchen table.

One day, attempting to undo
a summer's indifference,
he grabbed my ankles
where I lay
half-naked on the floor
and, whooping, dragged me

across yards of carpet
as a joke. Clumsy,
unthinking affection
that left my back a blister,
mother angry, and himself
ashamed, a wrong
he tried to right
with balsa gliders
and a kite that almost flew.

Today, my father
works oftenest
in his chair
before the television
(from which nothing
and no one can drag him)
reading books on how to
oil-paint, something
he will never do—
books that will join others
on his shelf: how to
whittle, how to play
the harmonica, how to
what have you.

This poem is about
how to make amends.
Step one is always to remember
before saying goodbye
to say hello.

CHRISTMAS MORNING

I turn again to old photographs,
the upstairs of our house
finally finished, floored and plastered,
where we lived then, the furniture
newlyweds could then afford pushed aside
to make room for a tree and toys,
to turn a barely furnished room
into Christmas.
                            My father and grandfather
bracket me, father smiling in a way
he rarely does today,
my wasted grandfather fat and vital
in his Christmas shirt, a cotton print
of pine cones and vague snowlike shapes.
Both sit cross-legged and intense,
assembling train track,
a transformer, freight cars,
obscure pieces of tiny towns and stations
littering the floor and table-top.

And here, then, is the only thing
that matters now: that they are pleased,
with themselves, with each other, and with me.

WHERE SHADE COMES DOWN

In a field of sun-bleached
green, of browning leaves,
one tree, an oak, and corn
stretching to all sides away
and above the sun, cut by
swallows, a dark hawk gliding,
a woman, my wife, beside me,
bees ochering about us,
beneath us flattened grass,
showy purple asters, goldenrod,
our blue shadows lost in
weeds and the branching dark-
ness beneath which we lie,
muted, earthen, neither
white nor colorless.

A DREAM OF STILLNESS

for Jordan

Gripping the stroller's sides, you sat
at first like a Fabergé egg within a basket
—a sentimental image, to be sure,
but we are your parents, and allowed.

As we drifted slowly from pool to pool
of shade, you cooing, just this side
of talk, of walking, your mother and I
just this side of middle age,

I imagined reading shelves of books
and drinking imported beer from China,
while your mother spoke of movies
she'd like to see, sports we might take up,

and you gave yourself up to our whims of motion,
your sleep-suited feet scissoring with pleasure.

POUNDIAN CONCLUSION TO AN OTHERWISE
ORDINARY DAY

The Down Syndrome doll we ordered
so our daughter will feel good about herself
arrived with the mail while we were at the lake.
She is a rag doll whose stenciled features
are all that justify her name: Dolly Down.

The accompanying booklet upsets my wife.
It says things I know enough to know
are things that should upset me—that Down Syndrome
is also called Mongolism, that adults with Down's
are like children who never grow up.

My wife begins to draft an angry letter,
while I go to the window to watch the five boys
who've come to see the fifteen-year-old girl
who lives next door. They want into her house,
though no one else is home, where who knows what

will happen. But for now they commandeer the porch,
swearing and shoving, smoking and posturing,
operating largely from the reptilian portion
of their brains. There is much loud talk
of beer and tits and how each other dresses.

Upstairs, my daughter is already asleep
with her dolls, though it is hardly dusk,
but she had a busy day splashing where the waves
just touch the shore. Soon she'll call
for a drink of water, then fall back to sleep.

Next door, louder talk of retards—friends
who aren't hip, aren't here—and pun-filled remarks

about one another's bodies, everyone pretending
more sexual knowledge than he possesses,
though the girl smiles in a way that says otherwise.

My wife reads me her letter, though the rage I feel
is directed next door. Yesterday they stole
the seed from the bird feeder and just now
started to fuck with my daughter's tricycle
until I opened the door and shouted.

Although they backed off, they laughed,
as though getting caught was, like my anger,
part of the fun. But they were pretending
more than they felt. My indignant wife
with her angry letter is happier than they are.

Carrying upstairs a glass of cold water,
I am happier than my wife, and my daughter
who will never grow up is happier still,
happier even than the fish who swim in the lake
and don't even own clothing.

LAKE GLASS

for Barbara

I have sent my sister down the beach
in search of buried treasure, and she
will find it. I know because I hid it
in well-marked mounds
and only just beneath the surface
(for she is little, and despairs quickly)—
small caches of colored glass
the waves have polished on the sand
until each piece is finger-smooth and singular.
These for us are jewels, a fiction
she only half-believes
(but this is a time when half-believing
is sufficient), humoring me
in return for my attention,
me allowing her to humor me
that I might please her.

While she is finishing breakfast,
I gather this booty for her
at the water's edge, where it gleams wetly
among pebbles and periwinkles
and stones just right for skipping,
until I have a rich handful. Then
I lose my find again for her amusement,
for she is at that awkward stage
(when does it end?) where joy
gives way without apparent cause
to petulance and glassy boredom.
Hours later, when we leave the beach,
tired and a little browner,
perhaps she takes her plunder with her,

perhaps it lies forgotten in the sand,
changed once more into broken Coca-Cola
bottles and other washed-up flotsam.

But now she reappears to drop a delighted handful
onto the blanket, then runs off in search of more,
her bare feet leaving small impressions in her wake,
her useless bikini top askew.
The pile left behind is glitteringly beautiful—
incandescent rounded scraps of an almost opaque emerald
    green
that like these brown and amber shards
(precious stones whose names we do not know)
began as beer and soda bottles;
small, glowing pearls
from coffee cups and shattered dinner plates
swept romantically enough maybe
from the galleys of swamped schooners;
translucent, deep blue sapphires (sapphires, we think,
are such a shade of blue);
pale green-white uncut diamonds
that mottle as they dry;
and best because the rarest,
mysterious wave-shaved rubies.

All this happened years ago, of course,
when the wishes I was called upon to grant
were modest, when pretty litter
was all it took to charm my sister
into pirate happiness. Now,
although she may still find lake glass lovely,
it casts no spell, and I
must look elsewhere for the jetsam
to lighten her boredom

and transmute her grown sorrows
into childlike joy.
These words are all I have, and they must do
(they are no more specious than those gems were paste).
Neither of us cares much any more
for hidden meanings, so
I will simply say to her, look here
to find some waif reclaimed by happiness,
a string of sunny, sandy afternoons,
a hoard of closeness in day-bright open spaces.
Redemption, after all, requires very little.
So take these gimcrack bits of glass,
a bloodstone syllable or two,
and leave this life awhile for the one you knew.
There is nothing so small it does not matter,
nor so marred it cannot charm.
There is nothing so common it cannot save you.

CHILDREN IN THE BEDROOM

We cannot keep them
out of here, away
from the mystery of it.
The three-year-old pages
through volume seven
of the *Interpreter's Bible*,
the kindergartener
fills out an order form
from a Victoria's Secret
catalog.
        They love the way
forgotten belongings
materialize here
unexpectedly, and the view
from our window, so much
more glamorous
than that from theirs.
They love the pictures
of and by themselves,
the scale, the mirror
on the door, the big bed
for bouncing or for lying
adultly still.

It was in my parents' bedroom
where we bounced,
my sister and I,
until caught, or snooped
for birthday presents,
or slept when very ill,
where all hearts-to-heart
took place, where mother

came to cry out and father
to sleep off their upsets.
And as though someone
were always upset or ill,
dressing or asleep,
the door was always shut
upon mother's musical
jewelry box, each bracelet
with a story like a charm
attached, upon father's closet
deep with the secrets
of old letters, suitcases,
and abandoned hobbies,
upon the muffled talk
of our parents' nonparental life,
the erotic quietude of it.

My girls are helping now
to fold a load of laundry,
struggling not to touch
the guitar on the rocker
beside the window. Soon
they'll fetch a book
or six and beg for stories,
or weigh themselves,
or watch me watching them
in the doorback mirror.
Perhaps one day
they'll write the letter
I never got around to sending:
"thanks for everything"
is all it would have said,
"I liked especially
the part where I was small."

THE FOURTH FACT

Birth, and copulation, and death.
That's all the facts when you come to brass tacks. . .
                    —*T.S. Eliot*, Sweeney Agonistes

Your father left this place a mess,
we certainly agree on that,
but I wonder if all our cleaning
and fixing up are really part
of readying the house for sale
or just some way of passing time,
something a father and son might do,
like playing catch,
and over which you'd have us linger,
as at your mother's, then
your father's grave you
lingered, as I shall at yours,
or you at mine.

           The work goes slowly,
deliberately. We find jobs that don't
need doing, and we do them—
reglaze the windows, scrub down
the kitchen cabinets—although
both of us know that one day more
is one day less. Last Saturday
I climbed into the attic, dark and grimy
as any shut and boarded mine,
in which we chanced upon your childhood,
or that part of it you didn't carry with you
into your next life, where we
became acquainted, while dust and damp
had their way with your toys,

with boxes of grade-school papers,
with a violin (unstrung, unbridged,
unbowed) that has not been played
since you were young, that has not sung
since you were a boy and sang.
For I cannot recall having ever
heard you sing. Even in church
when I was small and stood beside you,
the hymnal open between us, you
seemed only to mouth the words
that spoke of the things that last,
of faith and hope and love—and love
the greatest of the three.
Not that you did not, do not love me,
but that you did not, do not say so,
as I have not, although I grope toward
what I cannot say—here, now—as
Saturday, my knees straddling two
two-by-fours, I reached for boxes
just beyond my reach in your father's attic,
as I will reach perhaps for others
in your own attic's darkness.

But what concerns me now is what might seem
the least significant thing we found,
which even you, who want to keep everything
found in that house and cart it back to yours,
might readily have tossed away—a crumpled
bit of wrapping paper with a tag that read
"To Gene with love from Mother, Christmas, 1939."
Brought down into the half-light
of your bedroom, the paper was dingy
as last week's snow, in which
not even the most playful children

any longer wish to play, their snowmen
languishing in backyards where they melt a little
each afternoon, the angels they laid down to make
by flapping their cold, wet arms and legs
now indistinct depressions in the snow
across which they walk regardless
on the way to school.

                    Over fifty years ago
this piece of paper must have fallen to the floor
like one small flake in the blizzard
of a Christmas morning, perhaps melting
from your mind's green field even as it landed
and you turned to inspect what had lain concealed
beneath it through breakfast
and the long, sleepless night before.
Perhaps the package held socks or a sweater,
something warm and useful, or perhaps
one of these toys or books we just discovered
buried in the dark above us—
Pecos Bill and the Cattle Rustlers
or the Hardy Boys; a cardboard horse-race game,
or a kit for making soldiers of all nations
(complete with paints and copious directions)
to be gunned down indiscriminately
by a cannon that fired corks.

Whatever it was the package held,
as you bent over it in real or feigned delight,
your mother gathered up this wrapping—
and not because it was glamorously festive
in a store-bought way, or large enough
to save and use again. No, it was plain,
once-white tissue paper, the gift wrap

not of the poor, who use the Sunday funnies,
but of the frugal possibly, which your mother
was—the way she pinched and saved,
earning money selling Watkins Products
door-to-door. But this is not right either.
Your family was not tight-fisted
when it came to you, for you can recall
an annual small avalanche. And besides,
economy does not explain why the paper was kept.
But perhaps this is all wrong, and it was you
who found the paper as wonderful
as what it held, and who folded away
this scrap of the past to be found,
crumpled and yellowed, in dust and darkness.

But that morning the tissue was an expanse
white and pure as the neighborhood
beyond your bedroom window, where the storm
of a child's Christmas wish had blown into being
a deep new world that one might populate
as one chose with men or angels, in which
one might act out with snowballs or cap pistols
the adventure of Pecos Bill or the Hardy Boys—
a world, like this page, of possibilities,
like this soiled tissue across which
your mother left a sky of red and green
and silver stars, the kind teachers use
to reward those who stay within the lines,
to applaud children who know
all the state capitals, or the difference
between "principle" and "principal,"
or who can find all the prepositions
on a page of simple declarations.

Saturday, when you tried to explain again
why you no longer celebrate Christmas,
how your religion forbids it, I tried
to listen to your reasons, which made
the sort of sense such reasons do.
Well, yes, I said, and, Well, yes . . .
And I understand that everyone at least
pretends to understand. I know I do.
Pretend, that is. Yet today
I would ask you to look again
at this dusty, snowy field, this
constelled sky, this modest,
fragile souvenir upon which,
amid the still-bright gummed stars,
is affixed a tag across which a hand
has written, "For Gene with love
from Mother"—three simple
prepositional phrases, as you
would have known, even then,
as these bundles of homework papers
tucked among grade-school valentines
and works of art still tell us
(I see you were good at grammar,
though I confess some satisfaction
at learning you were not perfect, then).
"For Gene with love from Mother"—
is there anything else we long so much
to hear, that can do more to redeem
the time in which we clean house
and reglaze windows, play and grieve,
between our births and deaths?
It is as though for just a moment
we can hear your mother speaking to you again
across a distance vast as those

that separate the stars from one another,
a distance great as that which stands
between the heavens deep as a field
of fallen snow and us knee-deep
in boxes here below.

CONSOLATION AT GROUND ZERO

Because one can neither own
nor disown
one's own,
and because the same is
doubtless true
of time and history,
I suppose I cannot think it
altogether bad
to find oneself
at ground zero,
the children in your arms,
my arms, night
possibly just coming on,
and so
the baby tired,
fussy,
almost asleep,
asleep,
panic perhaps pulsing
about us,
or dulled disbelief
along every hectic roadway,
shop windows smashed,
abandoned cars
pointing every which way
down the now
vacant streets, as in
some science-
fiction movie.
    Meanwhile,
the four of us
would sit on the bed

looking out the window,
or upon a park bench
near the pond
where ducks
still
sport themselves,
squirrels busy
in the grass,
the fallen leaves,
the snow.
With what is to be
so beyond comprehension,
everything would remain
somehow
terribly everyday,
the wind
through the sycamores,
the sun setting,
the sky coloring,
then paling,
or storm clouds rolling in,
until
a millisecond later,
nothing is.
No time even
for pain,
for crying out,
for thought.
One moment
to be
intensely,
the next to be
nothing
at all.

The four of us
about to accomplish
what we
have always wanted:
to disappear
completely
together
without a trace
forever

from
The Lecture on Dust
(2007)

THE LECTURE ON DUST

I have come to deliver
the lecture on dust

(whose dusty notes are these?
whose ears are burning?)

when your house is burning
learn to love fire

a fiery phraseology my forte
ashes to ashes, I tell them

no fortress can save you
however crenelated, storied

past and future the same story
we live in a continuous present

—thus I make a present of awful
platitudes, grammatical tenses

their tense faces shining up
like sunlight on offal

lighten up, I tell them, face facts
or head for the doors

each is locked, to head or heart
doom's done deal, who struck it?

open your eyes: all thought
however striking, comes undone

neither first thought nor last is best
transparent eyeball, lifted stone

the stone in each chest lifts
splits, repeats: be mine be mine

the mined kingdom is now
and this is, this is, this is it

READING THE TAO

I wrote a poem filled with lies
about your hands, your voice, your eyes.

I wrote a poem that was true.
It didn't even mention you.

OPEN HEART

They are readying to repair
my daughter's leaky heart
that murmurs to itself
like a woeful manitou
watching the horizon
fill with ships.

They are coming ashore
upon the white expanse
of her stunned body, opening
her up, marveling, laying claim,
breaking what will not bend,
mending what they must.

They arrogate her brave
interior, cava and valves,
vessels, veins and cochineal falls.
They will bring back stories
we cannot believe:
Maskanako, Quetzalcoatl.

They are mapping her lush
interior, muttering like the wind
while she lurks elsewhere,
aboriginal and dazed and undivined,
not knowing if the man
whose hands are upon her

is the navigator Brendan,
who will find heaven
in her sacerdotal bones,
Brasail or the Paradise of Birds

in every soporific island
his bruised eyes touch . . .

or godlike Hernan Cortez,
working hard to staunch
the voices stinking in his ears,
hoping for the twin miracles
of wealth and fame,
and up to his elbows in blood.

READING *THE GINGERBREAD MAN* WITH MY DAUGHTER

Read, read, as fast as you can
is what I want to say but don't,
for that is what she is already doing
though moving painfully slowly
from word to word as through
something viscous as first
the old woman, then the children,
the horse, the cow, the cat
try to catch the Gingerbread Man.

She is at times a better guesser
than reader, trying
after a peak at the picture
to slip "stove" past me
where the word is "oven."
When I point to ask if that's
the word for "stove,"
she snuggles closer, grins,
says, "Daddy, I believe so."

Sitting on the porch,
we puzzle over morphemes
like two Talmudic scholars,
our reading as labored
as any fundamentalist's,
so tedious I wonder how
she can be following the plot,
its cookie-against-the-world
conflict, its paranoid's vision
of enemies everywhere,
its message of inevitable defeat,

of the brief ripple loss
leaves in its wake,
of indifference to how
the different suffer.
But she croons each "Stop! Stop!"
knowingly, like a seduction,
shouts melodramatically
the hero's brash refusals,
laughs at each escape.

She, too, right now,
would like to get away from me,
but tomorrow must deliver to her class
a report about this horrible story
she has been assigned,
and already, seven weeks
into this new school year,
her teacher, who knows
only one way to teach,
and the principal,
who has said he wants no
"special needs" kids in his school,
have given up on her,
are looking for excuses
to get rid of her.

And so we'll stay here, the book
between us, until the light fails
or we have finished,
although each time anyone
passes on the street,
she must pause to say hello,
to wave and wait for a reply,
which most of the time she gets.

When not, she squints, watching
some jogger or dog-walker pass,
her face screwed up expectantly,
her lips whispering
"hello? hello?   hello?"
until I recall her to our task,
encourage her to read more quickly,
enunciate more clearly,
as though by speeding through this book
she might outrun her fate,
as though a good report
will change the principal's doughy
smile into something real,
as though knowing which letters
spell "oven" will make true
her teacher's smiling lies
about the school doing all it can.

And so I urge her on
past another foe, the dog
this time, until a clique
of school friends bicycles by
and she must rush to the curb
to call hello. I try
to coax her back, shout
that we've just a few pages left,
but she knows how this story ends,
knows all about the fox
on the last page
who will eat the Gingerbread Man
because after all that is exactly
what gingerbread men are made for.

I yell, "Stop! Stop!"
imitating her, imitating
the old woman, the children,
the horse, the cat, the cow,
her teacher, her principal,
wanting to chase and catch her
so we both can run as fast as we can
and cry to everyone we pass
that they can't catch us.

But I sit, watching the girls
pass by. Each smiles and waves,
but no one stops,
and my daughter stands
a moment longer, arm up,
eyes following, hand moving
in a gesture of greeting
and farewell.

MY GRANDPARENTS' HOUSE

The operative words are dingy, unclean, depressing, grey. Cat hair covers everything. The tv trays are crusted with spilt food, the mahogany dining-room table deep in mail (Clearinghouse sweepstakes years old, newsletters from the Masons, solicitations from the Elks), the chair cushions stuffed with Kleenex, the hassock stacked with newspapers. The cat luxuriates beside the register; it is all they care to talk about: the cat did this, the cat did that. Grandmother lies fetally on the couch in a foul bathrobe, watching *Gilligan's Island*, the volume up, while grandfather, in yellowed underwear, teeth out, sucks oranges and waits for Merv on the one tv of four that works in the sunroom. The cat strolls sullenly about. Charro stars and is charming. And so we hate to visit, to shout over the television, compete with the cat. There is nowhere to sit that is not soiled, dusty, heaped. The air is dry, the hot rooms too close. But the last time I called, I remember how pleased grandmother was to learn we were expecting, and how loudly she laughed out of her small and breathless self when I shouted as a joke, "it's no big deal— what I did, almost anyone could do."

JULY 5th

Last night the sky blossomed with explosions, but they meant nothing and soon died away. Later, bottle rockets, firecrackers. I sat naked in the backyard with a bottle of my own and without fear of observation: I was that invisible. When I looked, even I could not see myself. Ffft. Bang.

Today, the heat continued. I drove into the country to fill a bucket with blueberries and to read the poems of Rabindranath Tagore, a few pages of the *Kural*. Neither was as blue as the berries, or as sweet, but both reminded me that everything worth saying has already been said and that therefore silence is not failure.

Now the berries are in the icebox, the books on the table beside the bed, but at 2 a.m. it is still too hot to sleep. There is silence at the moment and nakedness everywhere. I am on the porch, waiting for the streetlamps to extinguish themselves, for the berries to burst, for something to blossom.

LEAVING THE NEIGHBORHOOD

I am leaving this neighborhood
of shaded streets and well-kept lawns,
obedient dogs, disciplined hedges,
constant home improvement,
and cars washed every weekend.

I am leaving this neighborhood
that decorates itself each holiday,
where ladders are shared, scouts
knock selling magazines and candy bars,
and every little girl's a Brownie.

I am leaving just after the school bus has stopped
and the ChemLawn man has come,
just before the mail arrives
while the widower across the street
bends in his front yard puttering.

I am leaving this neighborhood
where behind each door people talk politely
of high-school football or the garden club,
and where, unless in a play,
no one falls out of love with anyone.

I am leaving this street of black squirrels
and birds at feeders, joggers and rollerbladers,
where my neighbor will shovel my walk
if he gets up before I do,
and bikes left out all night are safe.

I am leaving this neighborhood
where I never thought I'd come to live
and now cannot imagine leaving
because behind my door, off-stage, someone
has fallen in and out of love.

ROBBING THE DEAD

It is a dirty business. Looters disguised
as relatives haul boxes out the door,
like soldiers pillaging a secured village,
murderers disposing of the bloody shirt.

Sheet lightning and thunder like the ghosts
of bombs, but no rain cools the stagnant air
through which tools and lamps and ball gloves
make their way into the trunks of cars.

I look for something white to wave—
this calendar from the last good war,
this autographed ball, this sheet music
whose chords are all suspended ninths.

But everything I touch is yellow as the sheets
beneath the pale blue comforter
on this bed whose mattress keeps the shape
of someone now bodiless as a song.

The piano's keys are yellow, too, their hammers
striking the tense wires softly as the rain
that will not come, catching the apparition of a tune,
then dropping it. There is no one here to hear.

You got lost in a bit of lamp light, your white shirt
yellow against the sky-blue comforter, your ears
full of the sound of your own blood, of water falling,
of tools about their business, of ball meeting glove.

Silence draws itself out where I am, a taut
wire snapped by a slamming door, by the thunder
of someone hammering. Now darkness
begins to sing from each plundered room.

If this were a ball game, it would be the final
inning and, shelled in the eighth, we would be
without comfort with two out and no one on,
and all the runs we'd earned would have been stolen.

Your trunk of uniforms and battle souvenirs
is already gone when someone says, Take whatever
you like. But what? A ball of rain? A lamp
of lightning? This vase filled with thunder?

THE GREEN ONE

I live in the subjunctive, a world of if, perhaps, and could have been. I know the name that names my pain, have chained a line straight to it into sorrow's very heart. What is chained to yours? Hint: the last face you see will not be mine.

I confused self-exposure with self-expression, tousled hair with longing, parlor games for come-ons. Boy, girl. I was a guest on a talk show that nobody watched, and once made the evening news. That was me in the background wearing the embarrassing t-shirt.

You are in Paris, Marrakesh, Bali. You are singing pop songs in Serbian, writing poems to painters, drinking wine along the Seine. I am earning wisdom by mail, one mistake at a time. Power tools, holes in the wall, gin straight from the bottle.

Once I painted a wall where paintings were to be hung, large canvases in blues and greens, reds and grays. They were all about relationship, the painter said. Later I tore down that wall with a hammer and pry bar. It was all about recidivism.

Drunk, I call your lover but can't stop laughing when he objects to my tone. You are far across that lonesome ocean. I am green and you are grown up. What color does that make you?

Yesterday I spent an hour trying to tape your voice messages to me. "Move the blue one next to the green one," the painter said. The blue one; the green one: I love the way artists talk.

PLASTIC FANTASTIC LOVERS

Found after a storm upon the beach amid a pile of driftwood: a well-dressed Barbie doll and, unlikely as it sounds, beside her a small plastic statue of Michelangelo's David.

She didn't mind his nakedness
(she, too, was naked beneath her clothes)
or that he was sexually impaired—
for so was she as everyone knows.

She didn't give a fig for art
but loved to hold his man-sized hand—
just any Barbie with her Dave
alone where waves caressed the sand.

She knew that he could not care less
about her trendy clothes, her fame,
her countless glamorous careers,
or that she was a household name.

They lingered with wood enough to burn
if a cozy blaze were their desire.
If left alone they'll never leave
unless the wind and waves conspire.

But even if the wind should blow
and waves should wash them both away,
their plastic hearts will feel no loss
nor beat less fiercely than today.

THE MAN BESIDE ME

does not eat, but stares
at his food like a dog
at table scraps whose
smell is strange, head
cocked, mouth tight

the waitress passes
coos his name, whistles
a laugh, but he just
sits there, eyes
filling up with bones

STIR-FRYING

I am stir-frying vegetables—
whatever's cheap, in season,
whatever promises health.
Whatever I have.
                    I am fixing
enough for one, methodically,
doing it right, making it last.

I am stir-frying vegetables
because steaming was yesterday
and tomorrow. And as they cook they,
as the old folks say, stir memories—
of all the meals you threw together
from whatever we could find
in the refrigerator, at roadside stands.

Night after night, vegetables,
their storybook shapes and colors,
every night a different combination,
different spices, sauces,
each meal a virtuoso
variation on a theme.

Tonight, with salt and pepper
my only choices,
I am stirring vegetables,
wishing at least one came in blue,
at least one tasted like steak
or Scotch or, better, both.

I am stirring vegetables
in the wok you let me have,

the only pan in which I didn't stick
the girls' scrambled breakfast eggs,
the one in which, feeling gifted once,
I made curried shrimp.

You remember—
you said you liked it
surrounded by wedges of lime
on a bed of cilantro,
served with asparagus
and a bottle of white wine.

I am stir-frying vegetables,
but if you are free this evening,
I would be happy to run to the store.

WINDING MY WATCH

I am winding my watch
because it is an old watch
and keeps old time
of which I am fond—
the time of its making,
the time, just before dessert,
you gave it to me
to commemorate the passage
of twenty years' time together,
which was about to have its stop.

It is a thin watch,
which you said meant a good watch,
for you would have even our end
a work of thoughtful elegance.

I am winding this watch
that has outlasted, now, three bands
to show both
how permanent are last things
and how brief a time all things last.

A watch and its band,
once one, then two,
foreverness wed
to replaceability.

I am winding this watch
so it can pass
through its twelve stations
day after day
in its blind sweeping of hours,

its ceaseless sameness,
time heavy on its hands.

A ticking symbol of loss,
this watch catches at my wrist
like a small hand
that won't let go.

A PENNY FOR HER THOUGHTS

She could never
stand up to him,
stare him down,
talk back, talk bad.
He drove her crazy,
and that's no joke.
But for years
before and after
the drugs
and electroshock,
before she was dragged,
screaming,
from her home,
and after her demure return,
when upset she retired
to her room
above the living room
where no one lived,
until, eventually,
retiring became
her vocation.

And that is how,
grandfather ensconced
in the sunroom
before the tv
eating day-old,
half-price pastries,
their bedroom became hers,
where she sat smoking,
rolling her own
thin cigarettes,

muttering, crocheting,
reading Ellery Queen,
Rex Stout, until she
discovered numismatics.

After that, whenever
angered she'd roll
a cigarette and unroll
pennies, nickels, dimes
to squint at their dates,
their condition,
noting the S
that meant San Francisco,
the D for Denver.

Whatever else she did
up there
we never knew
and never asked.
But often when we visited,
above us we'd hear
the plink and roll
of dropped coins,
the creak of her chair
as she bent
over their magnified
minutia.

When she died,
and grandfather died
soon after, we sold
their home to two
do-it-yourselfers
and soon got a call,

were told we ought perhaps
to come over, take a look
at something.

          We went
to find the living
room ceiling partially off,
the floor deep in debris
with here and there
a green penny, a Mercury dime.
No one spoke
until the new owner said,
"There's a crack
in the floor upstairs,"
then reached up his hammer
to pull off another bit
of plaster and lath,
unleashing as he did
a small storm—tattered
slips of stationery,
matchbook covers,
torn quarter rolls,
all addressed to grandfather,
and each frantic with anger,
with cutting rebuttals,
fierce last words.

SHINING MY SHOES

I am shining my shoes
which I never thought
to shine before,
the expensive leather
weathered and dull,
dog-chewed, salt-stained.

I am shining my shoes
that take me now
up unfamiliar stairs,
into new rooms
in which people only think
they know me,
or know they do not.

To structure the days,
to kill time,
I create small rituals
with pots and pans,
calming bedtime books,
saddle soap and brush.

And so I shine my shoes
that those who knew me,
should we meet,
will conclude
that I am doing fine.
My shoes will tell them
nothing's changed
except for the better.
Old shoes, yes,
the same shoes, yes,
but never looking so good.

I am rubbing and buffing,
my fingers slick and stained,
wax like dried blood
thick under my nails,
so that having hit the road,
the wall, the skids,
I will not appear
to have hit bottom,
so that running or leaping or standing
dully still
in this dead skin
at least a part of me
will shine.

HOMELESS MAN IN MOM'S OPEN KITCHEN

There's nothing wrong with being bad,
he tells me, if you're good at it—
coming from nowhere to sit beside me
like a gift, a mirror, a payment due.

I was busy breathing second-hand smoke
and drinking coffee from a cup
still swiped with some woman's lipstick.
I was busy sweet-talking the waitress
into a free refill. Angel, I said,
but she'd heard it all before, here
where everyone could tell
what I was really doing . . .

And so he sat and told me how he lived
under the by-pass bridge,
how the police never hassled him
but stopped from time to time
to see if he was still alive.
He told me how he weathered
last week's blizzard and this week's
record lows in a sleeping bag,
snowmobile suit, and boots someone
had found for him God knows where.

We talked of shelters and waiting lists,
of how high the river was likely to rise.
He bragged he didn't drink or cuss
but confessed he liked Mom's coffee
and, when he could get them, Swisher Sweets.

Mom had some behind glass beneath the register
beside historic bars of chocolate,
dusty packs of Viceroys—
so I bought him some. Why not?
Because a man with open sores
on hands and cheeks
where the cold has cracked him open,
with hair longer and dirtier than mine,
who can, between the sentences we shared
speak softly to himself things
that shake him with laughter—
such a man deserves a smoke
and needn't worry about cancer
or emphysema, either of which,
or whatever lays him out,
may for all I know descend
like some bright, hilarious angel
laden with gifts
over which he'll laugh
through clouds of sweet smoke
and overflowing Maxwell House mouthfuls,
choking on laughter,
coughing bottomless cups of laughter,
until finally of everything he's had his fill,
until finally he's famished.

PAYING THE RENT

I am paying the rent
because even though
I cannot afford it,
the rent must be paid.

It is a small task
of grade-school arithmetic,
stamps and a pen that works,
two minutes at the desk.

The check I write is kin
to those that paid
for vacations, groceries, doctors,
your every newest hairdo.

The check I write
still bears your name
next to mine, and an address
where I no longer live.

The check is institutional green,
formal as our conversations.
It wants to know the only thing
that matters now: how much for whom?

Paying the rent, I write hurriedly
like someone checking into
a sleazy motel or signing
a false confession.

Each check is one more step
away from you, a letting
and a letting go, another month
in the nowhere of always.

PHYSICAL

1. Urine Sample

They treat my tiny cup of piss
like it was performance art.

2. The Table

One is now a country occupied,
another's occupation, another's victim,
the site of ultimate taboos.

One is now a code to be broken,
a sausage stuffed with sausage,
a shirt turned inside out.

One is now the definition of pornography,
a man without means, the voyeur's
wettest dream, the voyeur's nightmare.

3. Blood Pressure

The least of my worries.

4. Otoscope

A bug in the sluttish ear,
an easy penetration,
aural sex.

A lighted probe
down vacant streets,
along empty canals.

Where are the sounds of yesteryear?

5. Reflex Test

Proof one's responses are knee-jerk.

6. Tongue Depressor

The story: brief, tasteless.
The style: flat, clinical.
The dialog: garbled.
The setting: cavernous, symbolic.
The dominant trope: onomatopoeia.
The protagonist: wooden.
The theme: anyone can be somebody's fool.
The moral: avoid being French-kissed by a tree.
The point-of-view: second-hand omniscient.
The denouement: ambiguous.

7. Blood Work

No woman I have slept with
left me quite so light-headed.

8. Stethoscope

A wiretap on the heart,
covert intelligence,
one blind man's bluff,
a dangerous liaison.

Cough, and give yourself away.

9. Thermometer

Sometimes a cigar
is just a cigar.

10. Latex Gloves

For the prevention of disease
and the encouragement of fear,
a stylish but optional part
of the fetishist's ensemble.

(Don't you wish your parts were optional?
Don't you wish you weren't?)

11. Prostate Exam

I should, perhaps, have brought flowers.

12. X-Ray

No one has ever been so explicit
in giving voice to her desires:
she tells me what to take off,
how to pose and for how long,
when to move.
　　　　　　Not satisfied
with what there is of me to see,
she wants my bones, my cloudy lungs.

13. EKG

Further evidence
that we are the monster,
not the scientist;
not beauty,
but the beast;

further proof
that induction has its limits,
that there is a demon
in the box
and a ghost in the machine.

VACATIONING WITHOUT YOU

I am vacationing without you,
drinking bottled beer
and puzzling out crosswords
in a one-week summer rental,
walking a beach crowded
with families and men fishing,
but lost in a late fall evening
full of traps and victims.

I am trying to read a book
begun eight months ago,
but its stoic, blind protagonist
is barely there
behind the plot of last November,
its sadder story
and gut-wrenching heroine.

I am trying to take a picture
with the camera last used
when we vacationed
last year, but its focus
is stuck on infinity,
its lens fogged
with images of you.

I am wearing the shorts
I wore last summer, sand
in the pockets still from shells
you found and asked me,
please, to carry home for you.
I have them here, safe

and good as new. Look—
I have pressed them
like snapshots
between the pages of this book
with the happy ending.

INTERVIEW WITH A SUICIDE

You chose to gas yourself because . . . ?

Because nothin' says lovin' like someone in the oven.

Wasn't there something we could have done?

Don't flatter yourself.

Why did you do it?

Because the plum blossoms were falling. Because it was so cold on the Ring of Fire. Because my team lost and because all the pilot would say was that we'd be on the ground shortly. Because my girl left and now there is no here. Because the moonlight went crazy in the bedroom and the sunlight was so loud.

Did you make your peace with God?

No: why should God be the exception?

What can you tell us from the other side?

The bright light is a "No Vacancy" sign, and among those who come to meet you there is no one you were hoping to see—they all still want something, and they are never out of debt.

How do you want to be remembered?

That, I believe, is called begging the question.

Anything you'd like to ask?

Who was that woman dancing in my shower, naked beside me when the roads got dark? What was that sound that woke me every night, and who was the caller who always hung up? Why were the lights on when nobody was home? Why are the plum blossoms always falling?

SHOSHAKU JUSHAKU

Shoshaku Jushaku *means 'to succeed wrong with*
wrong,' or one continuous mistake.
—Shunryu Suzuki

I

One continuous mistake: to be the good son, good brother,
good friend, good father. To go to work, work hard, eat right,
exercise, rake the leaves and fix the leaky pipes. To row the
canoe, coach third, give up my seat. To sit zazen agreeably.
Not to attempt to be more than a friend to the woman whose
smile is heart's ease itself, not to cross the line but to say "this
far and no farther." To attend to the wise and tend the small.
To hold my tongue, hang fire, turn the other cheek. To be
prudent, reasonable, patient, forgiving. To be nice, to try.

One continuous mistake made with perfect single-
mindedness: but if that woman ever again says she hates
dressing up to go alone to the symphony, I will tell her that
I will dress up and go with her, gladly. Or, if undressing is
required, then there, too, I will say, I am your boy.

One continuous mistake: these hands that have done so
many nice, pathetic, futile things; these hands that long
to bring their emptiness to her form, to be mistaken there
continuously.

II

"There is no other way of life than this way of life."

I wait for your knock upon my door, concoct reasons to stand
before yours.

I hang on your words, in a gush of triteness tell myself stories about us.

What might we do that you have never done before? How long might I hold you before you felt safe, before you never again want to beat on the windows in despair of life's unbearable sameness?

I listen as you call me your buddy, tell me you cannot make up your mind. Clichés and soap-opera and illicit, unwelcome yearning.

This is my true nature, to be a ghost attempting to unlock delusion with delusion.

I know there is no other life for me.

III

"We can say either that we make progress little by little, or that we do not even expect to make progress."

This morning I awoke to an image of you beneath trees. I was not there. Your lips did not part for me. Your desires did not spell my name.

Thus I come closer to you, little by little.

When I have abandoned all plans, all desire, will I be closer still? Even now I search for you in the heart's bloody chambers. Thankfully, the blood is only mine. You are safe elsewhere beneath the oaks, the cool sycamores.

I care for you this much.

IV

*"Bowing is a very serious practice. You should be
prepared to bow, even in your last moment. . . ."*

Here in my final moments I find myself still falling. For you.
At your feet. For that.

I peeled my heart to lay it at your feet, then slipped upon it,
a would-be monk gone Chaplinesque.

Hungry for the space between your lips, for something to
light the heart's dim cell, I offered you a few words, dark beer,
jokes and self-deprecation. Desire's pratfall.

You did not laugh but offered me a story. The story was a cliff.
There was a sign at the top. It read: jump.

I watch myself fall from where I lay sprawled foolishly before
you, my heart going green, yellow, brown. From very far away
I hear my true nature calling.

Quickly, tell me your story again, that I might learn at last
to bow.

V

"If it really does not matter, there is no need for you even to say so."

It doesn't matter: it is all right. By which I mean it is not all
right. By which I mean that it is all right.

Where was I since we became friends? Dismantled in love,
away. Thinking you thought me awful. Your cynic. No time even
for coffee together. You thinking I thought you bothersome.

Sometimes my therapist. Then suddenly this. "You ask me something I can't answer right now." It is all right.

I sit here buried in fantasies, daunted, unable to find the off switch. To walk away. Knowing what I ought and mustn't but writing this, if not to sway you, then why? Bathos, banality: wearing sin like a ring of beauty, dreaming with tears in my eyes. Don't think twice, it's alright.

I will draw back into the proprieties of friendship. How are you this morning? How was your trip? Want a Good & Plenty? The right thing to do, but not all right.

Is it cruel for me to write you and want to talk to you? But what hurts more: emptiness or overfullness? Even if dumped and left to rot, aren't the apples what the trees had to do? But again, to stand at your door every day with more poisoned fruit can't be right.

So it is all right. Of course it is all right. By which I mean I think maybe nothing is ever all right. By which I mean I can't imagine it could ever be entirely not right. By which I mean it matters.

VI

"Even though you do not do anything, you are actually doing something. You are expressing your true nature."

We do nothing. Day after day we realize our true natures. Our nothing covers everything I do. I remain sitting quietly in my room. To leave, to move, to think would be unhappiness. I expect nothing. I am the stone for which the trees are just passing through.

I write you letters, this letter. Schopenhauer wrote, "If you want to know how you really feel about someone take note of the impression an unexpected letter from him makes on you when you first see it on the doormat." Were I doing anything, I would be wondering what impression the arrival of these words made on you.

I leave work early, leaving you a message that says nothing. Before you go home, you leave one for me. The next day, although Saturday, I come to work, wanting to see if there is a message from you. It says almost nothing, says to call if I like. So I leave a message for you, and later I call but do not reach you. We are doing nothing. We are expressing ourselves.

Last night, I listened to your latest message, over and over. I listened to you tell me nothing in a voice so soft, so gentle, so small that when you spoke my name it was not sound but a blown kiss. Or so I thought, so I wished to believe, but trying to do nothing. To hear you express nothing.

Your eyes, your demeanor, your true nature: I am not able to handle such complicated texts. I am stuck on your voice like a child learning to read. I know only the present tense and have forgotten what the word "friendship" means. No child ever wanted to understand so difficult a text. No child ever had so much trouble expressing himself. No child has ever been capable of doing nothing.

VII

"These difficulties gave me some experience, but it meant nothing compared with the true, calm, serene way of life."

We have shared private jokes, meals, a relationship rich in innuendo. We glanced away, stepped back. We showed each other what parts of ourselves were just the disguise. Now, on whatever log I squat, you'll recognize me.

You wrote letters, leaving blanks where the terms of endearment belonged. I praised your indirection, you my indiscretion. You kissed my shameful hand. I kissed your hair. You left me alone with your purse once, and I didn't take or touch anything.

I am wondering: what the hell's the deal with serenity anyway?

Tonight only one child is up late, wearing his usual disguise, doing whatever he is doing. He is stacking words like blocks and calling it poetry. He is playing peekaboo with what he pretends doesn't matter. Now he is recalling how, when he left you alone with his heart once, you touched but didn't take a thing.

VIII

"By purity we do not mean to polish something, trying to make some impure thing pure. By purity we just mean things as they are."

Because I do not listen for you, I hear you everywhere. Only if I look for you is this purity broken, only then do you vanish. Because I do not attempt to see you, touch you, I have no fear of losing anything.

True: at night I think of you until I become too excited to sleep. My thoughts many nights are impure. Night after night I polish these thoughts with no desire to purify them.

Desire was here before I felt it. Then I felt it and made its sounds. Now things with me are just as they are.

Perhaps one day I will find you at my door: how can it be otherwise when you are already and always here? You who cast no shadow upon this purity that burns so completely it leaves no trace. You whose absence means you will never leave me.

If you do come, you will not find me anywhere.

IX

"Knowing that your life is short, to enjoy it day after day, moment by moment, is the life of 'form is form, emptiness emptiness.'"

form is form &
life is short &
emptiness surrounds

in the quiet
bar-dark, dark
beer after dark

& you laughing
growing quiet
telling me

about your day
fragments
of your life

shared with plates
of food
another round

when it comes
when you lean
toward me

smile, reach
to touch
my arm

my hand
it is almost
enough

CALLING TIME

Rollie Sheldon holds a wristwatch to his ear.
Ralph Houk leans in to "help him listen."
Behind the crowds and springtime pepper,
they hear the sound time used to make in 1961.
It seems to please them, Rollie especially,
who must have thought he had a lot of time in 1961
when he went 11-5 in his new Yankee pinstripes,
fresh from college and D-League ball.
The year Roger Maris sent those 61 dogs hunting.

Time had a satisfying sound that summer.
John Blanchard got more playing time.
The time was right for setting records
that might last for quite some time.
Mickey, Ellie, Tony, Whitey—their timing
was right that summer, when time
seemed in suspension, measured only in innings
that were themselves subject to no clock
that wasn't wound by strong arms and gutsy fielding.

Ford Frick and endless talk of longer seasons
worked overtime to spoil Roger's record.
He could see it coming (he had good eyes).
Mick, of course, was always ready for the worst,
waiting on aching legs for injury's alarm,
spending the money he saw no point
in saving for some other time,
while Bobby prayed and Yogi joked,
and hot Rollie's watch ticked and ticked.

One evening, late in the season, running
out of time like running out a pop fly—

futility at war with hope, and nothing to be done about it—
Roger called time
at Tiger stadium, stepped out of the box
to watch a flock of Canadian geese
fly across the face of the sky's cool, luminous dial.

BERRY PICKING

I

The brief bushes hang heavy with fruit
that stains the plucking fingers red
the baskets fill and bleed

our mouths fill with pulp and dark, tart juice
our dyed eyes dart, bright birds
intent upon their brilliant foraging

thorns sketch on arms the face of theft
bees prick through branches webbed
and drooping, dusty, still as cloud

II

By evening, when recalled at last
each berry wore a gown of fine gray fur
we left them in the darkening grass

but what we took and threw away was not
what we desired, what we intended not weeping
baskets, bare branches, the aches we kept

but bending, rising, sweating, resting
we wanted day's green gathering together
the satisfaction of a mislaid need

YOUNG WOMAN CAUGHT READING IN AN
EASY CHAIR

Thoughts on a photo, circa 1948

Perhaps the radio was playing, perhaps not.
It was at first difficult to say. Everything
happened too quickly, and we were struck
by other details—the room's modest disarray,
the portraits framed upon the yellowed,
spotless walls beside the crisply drawn drapes,
the ivy twining beyond its pot like a fashion
disaster, an unsuccessful hair-do tossed
in tangled dishevelment across the polished veneer
of the usually stolid, typically silent radio
and over its sides, as though shushing it—
like cartoon ivy with its finger in a socket,
so shocked it seemed by what it heard.
How the plush easy chair in which she sat
wore like old pajamas a pair of frayed,
unbecoming towels removed only when company
was coming. And how this young woman
seemed not to have been expecting any, her hand
clamped across her mouth in mock chagrin,
genuine surprise, and a pleasure that could not help
escaping from eyes just lifted from a magazine.

Certainly, such details should have told us something,
as should her scuffed gray saddle shoes,
her anklets and dungarees, their cuffs
rolled up to mid-calf. As might the way she sat
sprawled across this chair, one leg

from THE LECTURE ON DUST

hooked inelegantly over an antimascaraed arm,
slouching as any parent would have told her not to—
especially when visitors might at any time arrive,
as we have, and the room moreover such a mess
("disaster area," one can almost hear
a scolding voice apologize), a litter of magazines
piled on her lap in a glamorous confusion
of fashion do's and don'ts, dating tips, and famous faces.

If we listen, perhaps we can hear what it is
that radio has been leaking into this cozy room.
Jazz, is it? The Hit Parade? Some soap?
One cannot quite say, any more than one knows
who may have entered this room with us,
catching this young woman so off-guard
to throw her into such delightful consternation.
It couldn't have been us she suddenly saw,
part of her mind still preoccupied perhaps
with Frank Sinatra, Rosemary Clooney,
for she was, beyond dismay, so clearly pleased,
and us she doesn't even know.
It was literally a question of who
she has eyes for, of who has been ushered in quietly
as an object lesson about always
behaving like a lady (to say nothing
of that get-up). No, it was not we
who had arrived hours or days early for a date
or something surely of this sort—
for she would not have been so disconcerted
had the visitor been a girlfriend,
nor so excessively gratified were the guest
merely a family acquaintance.

                One wanted,
regardless, to whisper (gesticulating laughably
from behind the new arrival, hands
a busy pantomime of cleaning), "Quick!
let's get this room picked up, turn off
that radio, hide those magazines, stuff
those towels beneath the cushion—and do
hurry up and change!" But it was already
too late for that, too late to do anything
about that hair, that "bird's nest." So at least
"Sit up straight!" (in which remark
she could not have helped hearing,
"what would people think if they saw you
Sitting here this way?")

                And for her
it is more than being caught unawares
by the photographer and frozen in just the pose,
the clothes, in which she would want most
not to be remembered. Look—
even her calves are blushing (though this is
partly from pleasure, is a part of her pleasure),
one magazine sliding embarrassed
to the floor to join the mounting evidence
against her, its garish paper voice
in chorus with the dungarees and displaced towels
taunting, "Yes, this is what she's really like!"
And everyone perhaps consents, although
possibly someone silently adds, "And better
than anyone could have imagined."
Except, perhaps, for Frankie, whose face
smiles up at us from the well-thumbed pages
of a magazine and who seems always to have known

all about such things as radios and movie stars
and young women left, then caught alone,
his approving voice having stepped softly
from the static-riddled speaker long minutes ago
to move easily as fancy about the room.

RIDDLE

Child's grave, Easter

Stuffed animals in the damp, evangelical grass,
dying daffodils and lilies, an unassembled kite
speak of love's promise, which does not stop.

Unable to stay, the assembled depart
to stuff themselves with promised cold cuts,
kite checks to Christ, and dream of flight.

But all such dreams are checked, stall,
fall to earth. We nose forward, unable to stop
the cut from bleeding or get the dark to part.

This earthen child doubtless won't take root.
Even the reasonable flowers for all their cold
beauty wilt, glum with their own conundrums.

The pink and yellow animals grow sodden
as day sinks beneath its weight of disbelief.
Somewhere old gone Christ knows why.

Puzzled, one might pray, root for lovely
answers, find some pink aunt or jaundiced uncle
to rehearse what green Easter is about.

Elsewhere, damp eyes cry uncle, beautiful
speech blossoms. This child within its hearse
of dirt knows neither dark nor doubt.

A CARDINAL

From gutter,
fence post, branch,
a cardinal
worries the morning,

cries above
his fledgling, left
in tatters
by the terrier.

Were Cotton
Mather alive, he
could say
what this means.

ONE TUESDAY

I

Heartbreak that can be told
      is not the eternal heartbreak

the Tao must be wrong
      about needing
            to be free
            of desire
    to realize
    the mystery

bent beneath desire
      I ride enigma's very train

II

Hearts that break are doubtless
      hearts that break
          that doubt
    bottom out
         in mystery, desire
desire
      name themselves darkness

without darkness
    no light
        no chance to know one dwells
    in mystery whose home
      is heartbreak
    whose city is here

In pain, indifferent to pleasure
  indifference to pain, my pleasure
   and my day
  seeded as the wind blows
  trained in loss

I am no sage
  rather refugee, castaway, child
  wren, sparrow, common mullein

I blossom less often
do not sing as I fly

III

How to use this heartache
  to stand firm
  to while away the hours

to let go of heartbreak
is to be wretched

I want only
  what Sappho
   wanted
   long ago
   on the Aegean:
  to sleep upon my soft
   girlfriend's breasts

IV

Not anthrax, plague
  the man who has my name

on some list
rubble and flame
raised fist, flown flag
blue of the departing train

heartbreaking
the doll pulled from wreckage
faces of baffled children, the call
never made, birds gone
forever elsewhere
your face

but not the eternal heartbreak
without name or place to be
set down
holding the shape of flowers
when there are no flowers

eternal heartbreak is not
what fills this page
is what these words do not conceal
is what they cannot say

eternal heartbreak
uncreates what is only made
lasts forever and helps
by taking everything

V

The sparrow
is a pretty bird
no city
is an island

if I write another word
I will never understand

VI

Heartbreak like water
finds the low places
easily spills
                or hardens
                            look
at how the lost
float, sport, drown
at how the happy recoil
from what is wet

on the Brazos
no more cane
no sun in the pines
only wind
four commandeered planes

then the sky
quiet   empty   blue
all of this and you
your breast
your face
and all the rest

POEM INTERRUPTED BY LACK OF LIGHT

I

Elsewhere rain blew in. There was nothing left to say, and no
one would shut up. Just a few miles away, newspapers were
repeating their dirt. We stood amid the gas station's well-lit
squalor, eating ice cream. We would have walked, but where
we were, there was nowhere to go.

II

             Here, where
        the split wood burns
who would think
        that this might be
             the last good time

             with war
and you
        growing older
             but for now
                  asleep beside me

             after how many pages
                  by lantern light
        of your book
             and mine

        the Northern Cross
             overhead
Lake Erie
        shushing
                  beyond the trees

from THE LECTURE ON DUST

III

When the coffee boiled over
        it was done
                hot, strong, full of grounds

good drunk beneath a moon
                busy washing out
                        night's bright clothes

your breathing steady and deep
                an echo
                        of the lake

your sleeping body
        warm, your face
                entirely beautiful

IV

the lantern
        dims, gutters
                campfire collapses
                        orangely upon itself

despite moonlight
                Aldebaran
                        shining
                                Saturn rising

the night quiet
        only the lake
                and something
                        in the underbrush

THE END OF MODERNISM

The sky hangs black in the pot's dark pool. I turn to offer you a cup, but you say you've had enough of stars.

Dawn: ice and sawed limbs strewn across the floor of morning, frozen ripples where angels disappear into the brine.

Why all this laughter amid so much debris? Your letters never explained, and helpless above the sink, I can only continue scrubbing these lines until they shine like some angel's wave-washed face, but chipped and crazed.

Down where the sky pours sympathetically into its cup someone is singing about the hangman's beautiful daughter, causing the chokecherry to sag, then break into pieces that sparkle like stars, like sea foam, like dishwater, that scatter like notes across this ancient kitchen floor.

THE BULL, THE DOG, THE HORSE

*. . . at times he shows us what the bull felt, what the dog thought,
what the horse was imagining.*
                    —*Constantine Leontiev, commenting on Tolstoy*

The Bull

The bull pities Ivan Ilyich and the man
who did not know how much land a man needs,
but is perplexed by all those Russian names
as he is when cowboys sing about dogies
or when the steers make jokes about bulldozers.

Eyeing the steers, the bull feels superior, cocky,
pizzle-ready for any teat-heavy, cudsy cow,
yet doubtful when he contemplates Leviticus,
Bulfinch's Mythology, or his place in history;
vaguely ashamed when passing the china shop.

The bull loathes Kansas City, Chicago, Spain,
grows anxious when children climb the fence
and threaten to enter his grassy domain,
approves of bully pulpits and bully boys,
Picasso, Merrill Lynch, Noah and his ark.

The Dog

The dog thinks *War and Peace* is bull,
prefers Charles Dickens and the slighter works
of Thomas Mann, thinks all thought
about what dogs might think is "bosh"
(such is the dog's way with a phrase).

When not absorbed with the Russians,
the dog thinks mostly about squirrels,
beef bones and strangers passing by,
his stuffed frog, closed doors, and how
the sunlight moves all day up the stairs.

In a brown study whose burden is fetching,
the dog suddenly entertains a new thought—treats!
how he dances for them at night, and how,
if on the sunless stairs he found us dead,
he'd bark until hoarse, then eat us raw.

The Horse

The horse doggedly imagines the most usual things—
pastures, steppes, Cossacks and cowboys,
Charlemagne, Custer, Crazy Horse, broughams
and Conestoga wagons, Silver and Trigger,
war upon war and furrow after furrow.

Glued to his imaginings, the horse improvises
the difference between "Turgenev" and "turgescent,"
imagines hack work giving one a charley horse,
fancies entertaining rumpy Anna Karenina,
the handsome Vronsky, along the Chisholm Trail.

Wondering what it must be like to be man's
best friend, to be cannonaded or gored, one horse
strays into a dream of a terrified small girl who,
clinging to his sunny mane, rides his ample back
bravely in slow circles all the way to joy.

MEN PLAYING CATCH AT THE BEACH

They have brought their gloves along
with the children and wives, girlfriends,
the cooler and blankets, as though
this is how a man tans.
                              They
are throwing the ball around,
calling a game in their heads,
pretending ease as they backpedal,
squint against the sun, sweat
as though still at work,
carefully indifferent to missed
chances, dropped cans of corn,
sending small apologies in the direction
of overthrows, behaving
as though expertise
were a possession not qualified
by performance.

                    They are so cocky,
proffering advice to the kids,
girlfriends they permit to play,
rehearse in gasps between catches
their sporting lives, shouting
encouragement to each other,
good-natured epithets that sound
like passwords.

                    After twenty years
of school, jobs and families,
they still have or lack what it takes,
still, by God, know how
to pound a pocket, throw a ball.

SHEKINAH

Crazed man passes a café where
at six tables in the sun
of a late afternoon in May
in our nation's capital, six women
sit drinking coffee

Windmilling his arms, he's after a
bit of God force, of brash
poetry, of sustaining passion—wants, as
he croons it, "to sex them
all night long"

They do not look up, they
do not stop turning the pages
of their books, do not stop
sipping, swallowing; indeed, they
now swallow harder

ARARAT FROM THE FLOOD

I

Now the man in the ash-covered coat
turns again our way, still crowing fire

& now something hovers over the still ashes—
it comes for the dove, for the sparrow

it comes amid the green airburst of spring
while sparrows wheel above the feeder

and in Iraq the few, the proud, are vandalizing Ur,
birthplace of Abraham, poetry, the wheel

as it comes, earnest doves in the streets of our cities
block traffic for a few crumbs of peace

with their block-letter signs and their wonder,
their chants and their heartbreaking satyagraha

meanwhile, the branches, terrible with crows,
are breaking, chance bombs explode indifferently

indifferent, too, the buildings as they crumble,
the pictures aflame on the walls, the birds

II

Now begins the sohbet between pulverized stone
and flesh, obscene terror and indecent empire

"lift the stone and you will find me" is what
the fliers of the missing say and say

"I have been away from my own soul,"
said Moulana Rumi, that rapt flyer, his words

still wrapped in the spring winds that arrive
masterfully one morning, vivant and scented

observe this scene: there are hidden symbols
and depleted morals everywhere we turn—

in the sparrows last seen in the lilac's bare branches,
the doves amid the shit and seed beneath the feeder

it is more than we can bear: Paula on CNN,
Black Hawks and Kalashnikovs, Saddam and Bush

today the bushes remain loud with birds:
what must happen to make us change our lives?

SPRING NIGHT IN KENT, OHIO

For Ginny

We here in Kent say sleep when the oaks sleep
and the backyard is quick with dark,
when the fast-food restaurants close and the dogs
that flank us on the couch have lost their bark,
when beyond our rooftops late Orion leaps.

But when the moon, rising above our street,
illumines the bed, and your hip and flank become
a refuge beyond some empty stretch of silence,
I cannot sleep or be of Orion's love-glum,
restless mind despite our two dogs at my feet.

How can I forgo in dreams the planetary night,
that sweeping orison between one day and the next
in which lilac and dogwood and iris open suddenly
and you await amid shadows like a sacred text
to be read by touch beneath a pale lunar light?

The moon gladdens the concealing oaks that rise above
all barking hunters and their dogs. In its glow
we are safe from the sin-sick world that sent us
upstairs sad, that lorn mirage beyond our window
behind which in Kent we lie fast awake in love.

THE LEONIDS

Our daughters drift beyond us.
They are growing up—sometimes
just another way of saying "apart"—
so are not with us tonight where
from a hot tub we don't mind

not sharing, far from them
we wait, watch beneath
a moonless sky so full of stars
it's difficult to locate Leo
behind the almost leafless oaks.

No matter: stars are falling
at a rate of 1200 per hour—
faint peripheral flarings, brief
pyrotechnic chars that cast quick
shadows, leave afterimage arcs.

Earth is wading what NASA
scientists call the "river of rubble"
Comet Tempel-Tuttle strews
across our path every 33 years.
Each November we enter it.

What happens then depends upon
"debris swarm" density, longitude,
and how the earth goes around the sun.
What happens has to do with how
what goes around comes around,

with how we long to be pulled in
by something and not drift,

with how we refuse loss, approve
the light, long for reunion,
for moments brighter than the moon.

After your blouse and jeans blazed
across my line of sight, and you
stepped into this tub beside me,
for two hours we weren't for a second
apart but centered, looking up,

working at 1200 kisses an hour,
300 for each daughter who is not
here to have her shadow cast,
secure knowing tomorrow the stars
will be right where we leave them—

the Big Dipper still pointing
the way to Polaris, the Sickle
of Leo, Orion with his dogs,
the Pleiades still two sisters more
than we have daughters.

Some nights we would stand
in this dark a long time
to see them again.
Unlike Tempel-Tuttle, their
reappearance is unpredictable.

They are here, then gone, then back.
We are left with the dust that,
not quite reaching us, showers
tonight with light—like some part
of ourselves we thought we'd lost.

Somewhere Comet 55P chases
its tail. We are at mutual perihelion,
and observing you by starlight
toweling off, I have a bright idea. Alone,
we seem to be thinking of nothing else.

WEEDS IN WINTER

—a book by Lauren Brown
a field guide
for blasted fields
                    the pages
the way pages get
when they have gotten wet
then dried

a present once
inscribed with something
about forever
on page thirteen
                    this promise:
"the plants have
by no means
disappeared"

II

my knees are stiff
as I walk to the feeder
atop snow a brief thaw
and a hard freeze
have turned to ice
past last year's chicory
the defeated tick clover
that can be known
by its hairy pods
    its lima-bean shaped seeds

some spilled seed
    millet, cracked corn
dances away

across spilt sunlight
into what is left
of the poisonous Jimson
the wild sensitive
    whose leaves fold up when touched
    whose pods spiral upon opening
where house finch and winter wren
    the inconspicuous brown creeper
    with its soft, lisping call
will find it

III

nothing is ever wasted
although nothing lasts
I've a lump in my throat
no one likes the look of

I've things going wrong
I didn't know could go wrong
& will soon be identifiable
by the scar on my neck

ultrasound, up-take scan, biopsy
but today I walked on water
at fifty, I am as old as DNA
as young as anything with feathers

crush me, and like the tansy
beside the fence
you will still find
some scent

New Poems

PREJUDICE

*Poets create . . . like diviners and soothsayers, who also say
many fine things but do not understand their meaning.*

— *Plato*

I don't like a poet with small, soft hands
whose verse pretends more than he understands,

who's written only the sort of poems
that never leave home without their combs—

a sandaled poet (wearing slacks, I suppose)
who carries an umbrella and can't write prose.

I like a poet in boots, whose lines
are stones no one mistakes for shrines—

a large-handed man with a battered thumb
(the nail gone black, the rest gone numb),

who lays down words like bricks in a row
and never says what he doesn't know.

REINCARNATION

The blue jay
hops from fence

to bush. He
tells me something

he assumes I
do not know,

then tells me
the same thing

again, more stridently,
and then again.

Were my father
not alive still

a few miles
from here, perched

on his porch,
I might have

to believe in
the soul's migration.

(UN)SEXY MEARNS

As I made love to you today,
I noticed that you'd gone away.
You never came because you'd gone,
so I withdrew since you'd withdrawn.

STAG HUNT

After a painting by Lucas Cranach the Elder

Beyond the window Mr Charlie's friends
are killing stags again while all their pretty,
terrible women watch, hands raised in witty
gestures of mock dismay (for nothing offends
these connoisseurs of carnage) as each beau bends
to fit an arrow into place, shitty
with hubris, or looses a leer he learned in the city
toward the garden his tight-laced mark defends.

As I say, to make it sporting, the men
are wielding crossbows, and the women securely guyed
underthings of many hooks that ride
across citadel bosoms (although now and then
undone by the strain of stooping) or through a fen
as swampy at its source as it is wide
behind—where horsey men have reared and thighed
their tumid way through stress tests one to ten.

Tomorrow's bloody schedule calls for a go
at boars with pike and blunderbuss. Unless
it rains, destruction will vie anew with an excess
of décolletage, the woods bright with woe
and silver mountings. Washerwomen in a row
will rinse the boars' blood from the hound's-tooth, caress
m'lady's funky drawers, and tunefully undress
each hunter with eyes that whisper, "mon ange, mon gigot."

If these merciless mammals glanced up the chilly
hillside toward where their castle squats, where sleek
and civil horses rear to the distant squeak

of a motet loud as Charlie, and as silly,
they would see me at my window, belly
pressed against the pane in rosy pique,
as the day falls to pieces like an antique
rebec made long ago in a shop off Piccadilly.

"Stuff and nonsense," says Charlie, who adds,
"you motto's 'live and lose.'" Not true, not true:
I've learned to hold my water and to follow through
at golf. I choose the finest gin. I've scads
of virtues listed alphabetically on pads.
I do the best I can; indeed, I do
better than that. Tonight, for instance, I'll debut
Te Deums for staghounds and a chorus of cads.

These pieces will play long after everyone
has dined and danced, and their latest prank's been played
at my expense: the fleche-courbe-sur-la-tête charade,
the possum fillet I am told is venison
or mutton, the chastity belt toward which I run
with key in hand only to find a shade
of eighty with scanties down and fat legs splayed—
a caprice I'll score for jaw harp, shawm, and gun.

But when the last trick rose has squirted, and the affair
has ended, I'll retire to my room to pace,
peruse Dufay rondeaux, and pray for grace.
Then sitting at my table in my only chair,
I'll compose a sylvan scene of a hunt somewhere
between chastity and bloodshed, a hopeless chase
wherein the gayest huntsman wears my face,
hums "je suis désolé," and is night's clear heir.

THE ~~SIX~~ FOUR EMOTIONS

Scottish scientists posited, by compressing fear and surprise as well as anger and disgust, that there are four, not six, basic emotions.

—Harper's, *April 2014*

I don't know how to feel about this. Either fear and anger, or surprise and disgust, seem to have gone the way of feelin' groovy.

Further: alert as I am to the world in which I live, I would have thought joy the Pluto of emotions.

All right, since you ask: sadness is Jupiter; fear, Saturn; surprise, Neptune (!); anger, the sun; disgust, the earth.

To tell you the truth, I hadn't known there were only six, and now there are but four. Is this what comes of too much television? Globalization? Secularization? The widespread use of prescription drugs?

Sometimes—like, for instance, now—science just pisses me off. Which I guess means it disgusts me. Today, three or four Scots—whose facial expressions one can only imagine—have left me unaccountably sad (although I admit a touch of the blues is sometimes a joy).

(Note: *Humintell.com*, whoever they are, claims there are no fewer than *seven* human emotions: "contempt" counts, they say, and I agree: contempt sure counts. Still, one wonders what they are up to, there at Humintell . . . certainly they are not keeping up with the latest research, regarding which, perhaps, they've nothing *but* contempt.)

Clearly, I am confused. If so, am I feeling anything?

What, by the way, of love, which I had thought a basic if sometimes hard-to-come-by emotion?

It would be sad if it were true, but maybe love is merely joy at first, disgust in the end . . . that, I fear, would not surprise me.

HISTORY OF A SHIRT

I can't remember just when or where
I got this shirt with its small tear
at the ink-stained pocket, the bit of paint
on one sleeve, the fraying cuffs, the faint
discoloration just here. It's had it, you say,
best turn it into rags, or throw it away . . .
and I would, but I like how it's made it
through the years, and I'm not persuaded.

This shirt, like me, survived divorce
when I feared I'd lose in bleak due course
my last, worst shirt. It went with me
to St. Petersburg, Mumbai, Helsinki,
had adventures in hotel laundries,
baked in the sun, riffled in the breeze,
hung in a hospital room when I thought
my sins had finally caught me. It's shot,
true enough, and will only get worse,
for nothing's as bad as it will be—the curse
of surviving, I suppose. Yet we manage,
this salvaged shirt and I, to stage
one more ragged appearance, outlast
another wearing day, frazzled but fast.

I SHOULD HAVE BEEN A PAINTER

I am a poet,
I said, and I

was hoping you might
pose in the nude

so I might write
a poem about you—

just a few brief
& stark-naked lines?

But she declined. "No,"
she said. "And don't,"

she added, "even think
of using your imagination."

DYING TO SEE YOU

I'd trade a year in heaven
For another day with you.
       —Dave Van Ronk

My great reward, not always earned, is each
night to lie down beside you. It won't, I know,
always be so. There are nights ahead will teach
one of us at the very least a thunderous no.

Unlike those loved and left in the past somewhere,
who never age or disappoint, for whom
we always feel the same despite the wear
of time and distance, regret's frail bloom,

you and I risk yet another night, and then
another day that may change everything,
and seldom for the better. Say amen
to that, and let love again sing.

I'll try to make it to morning admirably.
But because a story's middle can become its end,
arriving like a dark whisper, suddenly,
I'll say farewell for now, my truest friend.

At the risk of damping ardor, I will tell you how
I'll see you then if there is time for a last
fond thought—you will be in the rocking bow
of a small boat on Lake Louise, eyes downcast,

and wanting to be nowhere else, with no one
else, the day breezy, far off the descant
of birds. I'll drop the oars, finally done
with rowing, and hold your hand until I can't.

REFUGIUM

I wonder what you are thinking
over there, awash in yellow lamplight

while leaves hurry down the street
like restless orange and tattered refugees.

You are so preoccupied, and I
am so alone with this poem.

Outside, rain washes away memories
of things we've lost for good—

species, icebergs, last summer's madcap waves,
the clouds that yesterday scudded overhead

while we sat wrapped in thought
as in a comforter, with our

bowl of oranges, cold feet, magazines
explaining to us in plain English

why the bees are departing, why
the bats have packed their bags.

Tonight, my mind's in the mouth
of winter, icy with bleak thoughts

about when we too must flee,
the sky buzzing, all lamps unlit,

our thoughts caught in the branches
of the sycamore, the temperate serviceberry

for anyone to read, like poems
filled with small birds, white blossoms.

I THOUGHT WE'D NEVER GET OVER THAT FIRST ALBUM

Got live on the Zenta New Year, Detroit's Grande
    Ballroom, out on vinyl in January '69.
Less "sha na na na" than "no one here gets out alive."
High school almost done with me, believer
in the strobe-lit dream
(*it takes five seconds to realize it's time to move, to choose, to testify*),
in rock-n-revolution, Yippie sages, candle magic, Blake.
Ready to trip out with John Sinclair's
evangelical, alchemical, *almost unimaginable*
Trans-Love Energies White Panther *rama lama fa fa fa* freak-out.
Ready to *kick out the jams* with the bare-chested boys,
      brother Wayne & brother Fred, brothers Mike &
        Dennis & Rob
("music," sd. Sinclair, "*is* revolution").

Far left was far out,
& Johnny Rotten's bad-ass uncles—
    less ramblin' roses
    more handful of thorns, strung out
    & dangerous
    (*black to comm*, motherfuckers)—
Potawatomi voices from the whirlwind out of Lincoln Park
prophesying starship rides (hang on, *we're leaving the solar
    system*) & burning cities,
snipers on the rooftops, revolution for the sheer white noise
    of it,
pot, free love, & the end of waiting (*god it's so close now*).

        Don't take my word for it—the boys were "the
        counterculture at its most volatile and threatening"
        (Stephen Erlewine), "a catastrophic force of nature"
        (Robert Bixby).

Wayne & Sonic wannabes, we listened loud, *born hell-raisers*
& were transmogrified, glorified,
wanting to be both problem & solution
   (*This is the high society,* men for girls who *can't stand it*
   when you're doin' it right)
high on booze disgruntlement, on acid possibilities—
the future almost now, scary & exuberant & inexhaustible
   (the brothers played eight hours anything but straight
   at the Festival of Life in Chicago, August '68,
   the pigs in the street freaking out)—
punk seventeen-year-olds learning what we needed
from *The Big Us,* the *Fifth Estate, Crawdaddy! Rolling Stone,*
protesting the draft in front of the wrong building,
desperately sweet-talking every sweet young thing
(*I want ya right now* not the best come-on),
stupidly scoring oregano more often than not,
learning songs from the boys & Mitch Ryder, Terry Knight
 & the Pack
with a rhythm guitarist who knew maybe ten chords
& shirtless an unsavory sight to see.
But anyway & what the hell, our hair was right,
the blotter for real & potent, a few girls willing.

Come together, come together, yes yes yes yes yes

. . . . .

Today, the vinyl's scratched and obsolete,
Detroit in its dotage (*let it all burn*).
The dream, heaven knows, is over. Don't
look up the brothers in their decline, two dead
of heart attacks, one of liver failure.

Yesterday, standing on the corner
with no girls going by, waiting for

the light to change, I watched a car pull up,
music blasting from its open windows.

My first thought: "why's an old bald guy drumming
the wheel & singing along to the MC5?"

SPITE

Fair play may be an evolved response to spite.
　　　　　—"*Findings,*" Harper's *May 2014*

To begin, like a dull student, with the trivial, a definition: spite is "petty ill will or hatred with the disposition to irritate, annoy, or thwart" (Webster's).

Although apparently failing its audition for Evagrius Ponticus's 4th-century blockbuster *The Seven Deadly Sins,* spite, I have learned, is an important concept in psychology, theoretical economics, game theory, and behavioral ecology, among other intellectual pursuits. Spite is also the name of some punk rockers from Michigan, described as "hardcore" everywhere you look. There is, as far as I can tell, no punk band called "Fair Play" (though "Fair Play" was written across the abdomen of the 1940's superhero Mister Terrific). (Probably out of spite.) (By the way: what would "hardcore spite" look like?)

Sidebar: one can, of course, "cut off one's nose to spite one's face," which is (of course) to speak figuratively. There is a surprising amount of confusion out there regarding what the phrase means, though also a fair degree of consensus among internet authorities: to "disadvantage yourself in order to do harm to an adversary," explains *The Phrase Finder,* "to hurt yourself in an effort to punish someone else," according to the *Cambridge Dictionary of American Idioms.* But why is it always "yourself"? And why are most of the examples proffered concerned with me quitting my job?

Despite how interesting all this is, let us return to spite. Petty hatred, then, but not like hating broccoli. More like watching a stranger with a sack enter your vacationing neighbor's house and not calling the police. Whatever it was Fortunato did to Montresor in Poe's "Cask of Amontillado," it was probably some exercise in spite. What Montresor does to Fortunato, on the other hand, is not.

Spite, in short, is dollhouse malevolence. It was not mere spite built Dachau. That much seems clear.

The Goodwill store—where my father goes to buy second-hand jigsaw puzzles—is the sublimation of spite. The puzzle with one or two missing pieces may be spite in a box. But I am thinking about the petty self-loathing of noseless dolls . . . pieces of their faces missing like a puzzle lacking a patch of sky, the table showing through. Does that flesh out (ha ha) a definition?

The study *Harper's* so neatly summarized was written up for *Science Daily*, which tells us that, according to Rory Smead and Patrick Forber (both, I take it, professors of philosophy), "fair play" is not mere selflessness but a strategic response to spite. "Fairness," I read, is "a strategy for survival" in a world rife with spite. A modified version of the "ultimatum game" was used, but I won't bore you with the particulars. As for spite itself: it apparently doesn't need to be accounted for.

1 Samuel 2:31-32 (New International Version): "The time is coming when I will cut short your strength and the strength of your father's house, so that there will not be an old man in your family line, and you will see distress in my dwelling." Given how much worse this could have gone, is the House of Eli about to reap merely the spite of Jehovah, whose nose is clearly out of joint?

"Never underestimate spite as a motivator for genius," writes Sam Keen; "I like to write when I feel spiteful. It is like having a good sneeze," D.H. Lawrence confessed. "My talent was the uncompromising ability to feel spite," brags Natsuo Kirino.

When "spite" in the sense of something that simply "induces vexation" (*Collins English Dictionary*) is combined with its sense of "a need to see others suffer" (*Memidex.com*)—any others, unknown others—then we get car remotes that sound the horn, mail from the Publishers Clearinghouse, low-calorie beer. And I must ask myself: have I written this out of spite or to spite spite? Does fairness enter into this at all? Have I lopped off my nose to spite my prose?

DEFINITION

A prose poem should be square as a Picasso pear, or paragraphed like that same pear halved, then halved and halved again—free as air, palpable as an air crash and as final, yet somehow not all there.

A prose poem should be neither short nor long and somewhere between a snort and song. It should be dense and chaotic as a World Series crowd, yet open and orderly as the game being watched. It should be loud as the nameless lost are loud, quiet as a mugger in moonlight, magical as the maniac's ghostly knife, mundane as the victim when finally found. A prose poem should be shocking as the unspeakable when spoken is shocking—and as familiar.

Its feet all thumbs but with every line justified, marginal because it knows where the margins are, intimate with disinheritance, the prose poem's job is to follow its nose, accepting all comers, admitting defeat.

The porcine prose poem speaks: "waste not, want not" and "learn to live on garbage and in mud" it tells us straightforwardly when it stops you in a crooked street to hand you a slippery pearl, a bitter sweet.

In *Streetcar Named Desire*, the prose poem plays Stella. And Blanche. And Stanley. In *My Fair Lady*, Eliza Doolittle: make of me what you will, it says; make me and I'll make you, it thinks.

For all its history and intellect, a few dirty secrets and neglect. For love, the French.

Not equal to or better than or worse; neither prose nor verse; perhaps not for you or me.

OLD TOOLS

HAMMER W/ SCREWDRIVERS

It is metal, the handle brass, the clawed business end steel. It is eight inches long and good for hammering I don't know what. What makes it special is that the handle unscrews to become a flat-head screwdriver. The end of that screwdriver also unscrews, revealing a second screwdriver (flat-head again) whose end likewise unscrews to reveal a third (ditto), in the handle of which is a fourth, tiny screwdriver ideal for tightening the screws in eyeglasses. I borrowed this utilitarian matryoshka doll perhaps forty years ago. It belonged to my father, and I never gave it back, even though one can be purchased to this day for $22. Perhaps for a while he looked for it, then gave up—one more thing lost in the disaster that is his basement. I keep it in my toolbox although there isn't room for the tools I use all the time. This, I never use. I would say that I don't need it, but that wouldn't be true.

OIL CAN

It's made of copper. Its reservoir holds perhaps half a pint. It belonged to grandfather, and the oil it still holds has been in there at least thirty years. Beneath it, a slow stain darkens a corner of my workbench, and the screw-on spout needs oiling; it won't come off, though I can't say I've ever tried very hard. I never use the thing, keep it for sentimental reasons, a leaky memento mori. I suppose he used it to oil his lathe, drill press, to loosen recalcitrant nuts. I recall us in his driveway, oiling my bicycle. I remember standing in his basement while he took from the window sill above the belt sander the 19¢ bottle of iodine with the skull and crossbones on the label, smarting the cut I got fooling with the kickstand. Palpating the bottom of the can had made a small thumpa thumpa sound, like a heart briefly beating.

ADJUSTABLE SQUARE

This I've had since square was the last thing I wanted to be. It looks just like a Mohawk Shelburne 12" for sale on ebay and described as "vintage." Mine, however, is probably older and was made by L.S. Starrett of Athol, Massachusetts. Starrett, I learn, is a company whose "products are well known among machinists and tool and die makers," which grandfather was. The ruler is inscribed with the company's logo and marked "Hardened No. 4." Don't ask me what that means. I have used it to cut mat boards, to get a straight line started when cutting drywall. The bubble level lost its bubble long ago. Grandfather lost the whole damn thing long ago. I am still adjusting—to loss, to living life on the square, to going straight. It is not for nothing the level doesn't work. These days, I keep it in the bottom of the tool box, buried beneath some old rags, which I stupidly think will keep it from ever getting bent.

PRY BAR

Another tool from grandfather by way of my father. I used it to tear up two layers of linoleum and a subfloor in my kitchen, to lift the large slabs of granite edging the patio, so I could dump gravel under them to raise each a couple inches and stop the flower beds from flushing dirt onto the brick in heavy rains. It's short but heavy and was originally a battleship gray, but that has largely worn away. It has a pleasant, functional shape, hooking at one end—the end notched and excellent for coaxing loose well-pounded nails—bending slightly outward at the other, away from the hooked end. Like a baseball, it feels good to hold, to joggle. It was made to be abused. No manufacturer put his name on it, disowning both it and the work it would do. Still, it is worthy of being painted by Jim

Dine or bequeathed to the Whitney to be hung just as it is. If I lived in a more dangerous town, I might keep it by my bed to brain intruders. Instead, it hangs out in the basement on a hook in the pegboard. Were one to pry into its private life, about what might it be dreaming? Of all the nails whose heads it has mangled and torn off, and the delight therein? Of how attractive the cross saw looks at evening in the dimming light coming through the grimy windows? Of the night it spent in the uncut grass, too heavy for any rain to wash it home?

MITER BOX

It's old, made by my grandfather I don't know when and inherited by my father when grandpa died. I know from old photographs that he and father used in when, beginning in 1953, they built the house I grew up in. For the past several years, I've borrowed it whenever I had trim to cut. The last time I came to fetch it home, father told me to keep it, he didn't need it back. Which was to say that he was old and wouldn't be doing any more sawing in this life. The box was made of scrap wood and is plenty gouged and beat up. Its sides wobble a bit, and the saw is dull as hell. I imagine grandfather making this box. I think about the things he made using it, the things my father made. I recollect what has happened to those things, and when I do, I grow a mite wobbly and think this saw may be dull, but it still can cut.

HAND DRILL

It looks like something the Amish might use. It looks like it belongs in a tool museum. A crank or brace with handle, at one end the head or knob, at the other cam ring, pawl, ratchet, chuck. Nothing special. In the Cape Cod divorce was causing me to vacate, the previous owner had finished off the upstairs all by himself, and every move he'd made was rinky-dink, one closet doorless, the frame of no standard size. To keep busy, I was taking care of some deferred repairs and improvements and drove a door to my father's to cut it down on his table saw. He volunteered to return with me to help hang the door, which would prove, he promised, trickier than I might think. We chiseled the hinge and latch slots, then I measured the doorknob, father locked a bit in the chuck, and I cut the hole, which proved too small. Father apologized . . . he must have inserted the wrong bit. "Have I become that pathetic to you?" I asked, cranking the drill in slow, jerky revolutions, the empty chuck pressed against my chest. It was time to take father and his drill back home. It was time for both of us to leave.

CLAW HAMMER

This one means business. Heavy, deadly. My initials on the ash handle. It's one of thirty or so hammers distributed chaotically about father's basement and garage—ball pein, tack, sledge, straight pein, brass, watchmaker's, rawhide and rubber mallets, pin, club, claws of all shapes and sizes—his and the ones he inherited from his father. Despite being so numerous, the one wanted can rarely be found. This one, I appropriated long ago. It reminds me of a story—about a couple in their sixties who lived down the street from my parents, the husband coming up from his basement one day to beat his wife to death with a hammer. Visiting my parents soon afterward, I listened to mother say how, at church, someone had jokingly asked if she were worried dad might do the same. She'd said she wasn't. "Because you know how much I love you," dad jumped in. "No," I said, "because she knows you could never find a hammer in that basement." Ball pein, tack, pin, club, joke.

BASIN WRENCH

If I had any brains, I'd call a plumber. Using this, I am Procrustes on his bed, Phalaris in his bull. Surely, it was passed along by father as a joke. After wrestling the wrench into place, invariably I find its jaws clamped to turn in the wrong direction. Of course it is dark under the sink, and the propped flashlight of course keeps falling over. If my current faucet problems continue, one day you will soon find me wedged between the drain pipe and garbage disposal, a can of Comet, bottle of Windex, piles of empty plastic bags scattered about my now-lifeless feet, still clutching the shaft and T-bar. I will have assumed a position usually reserved for torture victims and sexual deviants. Check your Plato, Kant, Hegel, Heidegger: not one good word directed toward the basin wrench in the entire history of philosophy. Check Homer, Dante, Shakespeare, Goethe: again, not one affirming reference. Even Dr. Seuss, that usually affable soul, gave vent to this:

> I hate this tool in every way!
> I hate it every single day!
> Fuck its T-bar, fuck its handle,
> Fuck it with a roman candle!

Let the basin wrench try to unscrew that.

CROSS-CUT SAW

A Disston Keystone K-6 Challenger. The darling of the pry bar's eye (the pry bar likes 'em dull; the pry bar likes a challenge). Into the apple handle three sprigs of what might be honey locust have been carved, or maybe grass gone to seed. Although I've used it countless times, I suspect the geniuses on *CSI: Miami* could still find on it somewhere grandfather's fingerprints. It's there in the old photographs of our house being built, odalisque of the tool set, lying languorously here and there, brazenly riding the saw horses, giggling with the hex wrench. Naked, seductive (albeit tarnished) steel heel to toe and front to back; insolent come-hold-me handle. Although I cannot "play" the saw, it sings an ancient call-and-response each time I use it, a song of 2 x 4s and give-and-take, sawdust and grandfathers.

THE THREE GREAT IDEAS OF YACOUBA SAWADOGO

"My father is buried here,"
Sawadogo says, a hatchet slung
over his shoulder, sitting among
his cows, guinea fowl, goats,
beneath acacia and zizyphus trees
in Burkino Faso, western Sahel.
Unlike others, he could not
abandon his farm. "My father
is buried here," he says.

He cannot read or write
but fancies himself an innovator.
In the face of years
of hotter, drier days, he
"revived a technique local farmers
had used for centuries," digging
shallow pits—*zai*—to concentrate
what rain fell: his first
idea an act of remembering.

Yacouba Sawadogo's second idea was
tossing manure into the *zai*.
Neighbors mocked him— he was
wasteful, they said—but millet
and sorghum grew in greater
abundance, saplings sprouting from seeds
in his animals' shit. Letting
the trees alone, not uprooting
them, was his third idea.

As they grew, so did
crop yields. Trees buffered wind,
kept seeds from blowing away,
anchored soil, shaded the young
millet and sorghum, the livestock,
the people. Fallen leaves provided
fodder for cows and goats,
mulch. The trees provided medicines,
firewood (enough, eventually, to sell).

"Since I began this technique
of rehabilitating degraded soil, my
family has enjoyed food security
in good years and bad,"
boasts Sawadogo, scratching his beard.
His ideas have spread across
Burkino Faso, Niger, Mali—now
the greening of the Sahel
is visible from outer space.

Says Sawadogo, "I've used my
motorbike to visit about a
hundred villages, and others have
come to visit me
and learn. I must say, I'm
very proud these ideas are
spreading." Such farming is free,
and "the more trees you
have, the more you get."

Says Oumar Guindo, a Malian
farmer, "before, this field couldn't
fill even one granary. Now
it can fill one granary

and a half." Says another,
"before, most families had only
one granary each. Now they
have three or four, though
their land has not increased."

In Niger alone, 200 million
new trees, 12.5 million acres
rehabilitated. Water tables have risen
5-17 meters. "My conviction,"
Says Sawadogo, "is that trees
are like lungs. If we
do not protect them, increase
their numbers, it will be
the end of the world."

TWO FOR KO UN

1.

the garbage
is undisturbed

the dogs
grow forgetful

2.

snow and
nothing but
snow, then

a feather

drifting down

SNAPSHOTS OF CHINA

1. Upon Being Asked to Go to China

If I wanted
to visit China

I would go
to the Great

Wal-Mart store—
my first thought

2. Poem at the Foot of the Great Wall

Renaud translates:

"Only the good
man makes it
all the way"

I stop climbing
after 1000 steps
make it back
all the way

3. For Pratim

Along the Wall
you ask one
question, then another,
but my ignorance
is as great
as this winding
wall is long

4. *Smoke*

Caught in traffic
my driver offered
me my first
cigarette in years

I left my
ashes in Beijing

5. *Mr Li Jing Rui*

At our welcome dinner
with the senior editor
of the *Guangming Daily*
I struggle with my
chopsticks until he notices
& requests two forks

6. *Busy Beijing Afternoon*

I watch three willows bow
To a stiff March breeze

7. *Cold Reflections*

Trying very hard to be spiritual,
I am distracted by a man
who observes that the Aroma Pavilion
is next to the men's toilet

8. *The Square Pond, Prince Gong's Mansion*

Geese on the pond
—always now

for them, no yesterday
no tomorrow

9. Sign at the Summer Palace

"Mind the Hilly Road"

Yes—

Mind: the hilly road

10. The Chinese Keats

A man writes poems
on the stone walk
with mop and water

11. Out Walking

Unlike Li Po
I, wandering
T'ai Mountain,
watch geese
disappear but
cannot write
one word

12. Summer Palace

A magpie cries, takes
flight, becoming a speck,
then less than that,
leaving only magpie cry

I count my yuan,
but it has flown,

leaving behind a meal
& this small poem

13. On a Street, Xi'an

A man takes my photograph,
rubs his chin to indicate
my beard and smiles, nods
thanks, smiles again, nods again

Now, two girls want their
photo taken with me—Renaud
says I look to them
like a movie star . . . I
make plans to move here

14. Forbidden City

Terror lurks still
in the Eight
Banners' armor

15. Temple of Heaven

The air in Heaven
   is wretched,
but the blessed are
   not deterred . . .
Eternity is sing-alongs,
   pipas, dominoes

16. Terracotta Warriors

6000 warriors still guard
Q'in Shihuang . . . a few
have lost their heads

during the past 2000
years of unfurloughed duty

such loyalty in this
clay graveyard, battle formation
of giant toy soldiers
like heaven's basement or
the attic of hell

17. Bust of Archaic Archer

More loyal than you
more real than I

18. Norm

Ah, today Norm
is the sick
man of Asia

19. Snack Stand

Two birds
peck at
seeds spilt
beneath a
stall—
    some
have sprouted . . .
the seeds
I mean

20. Outside Cloud Mountain Nunnery

Quail eggs and weak tea
Car horns and temple bells
Smell of smoke, incense, cabbage

21. Tomb of Lao Tzu

Rain last
night, today
I leave
two footprints
at old
master Lao
Tzu's tomb

22. Taoist Monastery

I give a young monk some incense sticks
he gives me a bite of his lunch

around another corner, an old monk says hello
as last year's leaves scatter . . . it is enough

23. Hotel, Hongzhou

From the eighth-floor window
of my five-star hotel
I look down on one
of the city's smaller dumps—
everywhere there is a poem
awaiting its two poets

24. Easter in Hongzhou

Even Norm
has arisen

25. A Walk in Shanghai

So many people
in dire need

keep the streets
& sidewalks spotless

26. Ginny, You Are Not Forgotten

Not gone so very long
yet each day I think
more often than the last
of your arms, the mouth
that wishes to kiss mine

27. Lingyin Temple

I did not
find the Way
although I did
with regret find
the way out

28. Another Photo Op

Two more women
want their picture
taken with me

Renaud laughs, asks
for my autograph

29. Incorrigible

Norm says
the jellyfish
tastes like
peanut butter

30. International Call

Shanghai to
Kent, Ohio:
money talks

31. En Route

From the riffled leaves
    of Renaud's book
on Ming Dynasty furniture
    fall the orchid
petals left on last
    night's cool sheets

32. "Shanghai School"

No one in Ren Xiong's
Thatched House Beside Fanhu Lake
just an empty home, planted
fields, a road, one heron

33. Xi'an to Hongzhou

Rivers, mountains
Mencius & Moutai
before & after

34. Yunxiu Nunnery

Finally tired of tramping
the street of Shanghai
I return to where
I have never been

35. In Hongzhou

Beside the lake
I read the poems
of Mao Zedong

"by lakeside grievous
water flows along
with the crowd"

with Phil Ochs
I ask, was
this the enemy?

"I sigh to see
Deep water under
Deep blue sky"

36. In Shanghai

A Chén Hóngshòu landscape
retouched by city planners

37. Residence of Zhou Enlai

Sign
beside the exit

reads
"to be continued"

38. Left Over Breakfast Roll

The sparrows
to whom

I throw
a crumb
don't care
that they
are Chinese

39. Yuyuan Garden

Wildflowers find
roothold, read
the carp

40. Last Night

Nothing people do
that doesn't happen
on these streets—
the body breaks
before the soul

41. Shanghai Honky Tonk

On the way
to the airport
my driver plays
the Hank Williams
I gave him
and we both
try singing along

"TEAM UP WITH JESUS"

reads the sign
outside a church
that seems at home with kitsch

& I would except
He umps the games
& always gets to pitch

JOB'S DREAM

I dreamt I was Jehovah's mutt
gnawing the bone of some mistake
waiting for Him to scold
make me beg, speak, roll over

Or perhaps, finding me diverting myself
with power drill, tax form, violin
order me to play dead
or dance for a tossed treat . . .

Shaking the sleep from my eyes
& the dream from my head
I remember: "creation is templed"
see the cookies on the plate

NOTES ON A WREN

I don't know what kind of wren it is (if wren it is), comes to
the feeder every day. There are too many kinds in my book of
birds, most, to me, almost indistinguishable from the others.
I'm also not sure why knowing the correct name matters.
Doubtless, it matters more to me than to him.

Him? Why do I think I know this?

Pecking seeds or hopping about the maple, he arrives each
day only after the cardinals have departed. Which seed he
prefers, I can't say, although I'd like to know.

Today he flew from the filled feeder to the broken feeder
that dangles from the redbud. He looked about him, left, and
a moment later returned to the broken feeder. He was like
some avian inspector, preparing to write me up.

If there when I go out with a bowl of seed, new block of suet,
he moves away slightly and watches impatiently. I am the
slow waiter for whom he'll leave no tip.

Wren: all I know is the word.

REDBUD

redbud planted the summer
we planted ourselves here

redbud, now ten years
rooted in this spot

redbud that each spring
you say is dead

& each spring is not

BECAUSE OF THE SNOW

what has been covered
can now be seen

STILL LIFE WITH LAMP AND DOGS

Pillows covered in vines
& flowers
rest upon the armchair

They must have lain
so awhile
they are so overgrown

Two grey pillows on
the couch
like rocks on rocks

Two dogs, one per
pillow, one
dog dreaming, one awake

As for the lamp
who knows?
in the corner chanting

its mantra: Let there
be light,
let there be light.

COURTSHIP IN WARTIME

My father was drafted
got sent to Germany

complained about warm beer
took pictures of castles

His rival, Don, enlisted
got shipped to Korea

sent home letters filled
with dirt, horror, death

Mother chose my father
the castles and beer—

there'd be time later
for horror and death

HOARDING

For years before he died, grandfather kept,
stacked in his basement, every can, every
lidless jar and pastry tray that came
his way—bags (paper and plastic) stuffed
with bags, grimy pyramids of crusted bottles.
He had already filled one workroom wall,
floor to ceiling, with cigar boxes heavy
with carefully sorted screws, bolts, washers, drill
bits, hex wrenches, solder, sandpaper, and such.

Easy to guess what he saw coming,
harder to say why so many torn
sacks, bent trays, and pickle jars would
be required. Perhaps it was just habit,
a grasping refusal to acknowledge the end
of needing, wanting, using—why, I guess,
my father still holds onto a boat
he keeps in the garage and hasn't
put in the water for fifty years.

Perhaps grandfather hoped that what was coming
could be put by for a while.
After he died, we found our presents
to him—sweaters, gloves, ties—still swathed
in tissue in boxes under his bed,
as though he'd concluded that his life
was already over, or that a next
might require new clothes. As though believing
that those who have saved will be.

WALKING THE BEACH

The beachgrass is bowing to its shadow:
in greeting or farewell? Who can know?

The grasses grip the dunes: Passionately?
Desperately? Indifferently? At the shoreline
some child's pathetic Stonehenge crumbles.

There are precious few birds, a few footprints
soon erased by the melancholy grating of the waves.

I'm only calling this "beachgrass." I'm not sure
what it is, don't know if this over here is wild grape,
what fish these bones belonged to.

This fresher fish the storm last night surprised—
catfish? drum? walleye?—interests the gulls.

I, too, have an interest in things dead, things losing out—
coral, small frogs, little brown bats—
but I don't any longer care to know their names.

They leave behind less than the long gone teenagers
who carved their initials into the breakwater back in '58.

Meanwhile, that child's sandy morning labor—
her Yamatai, Carthage, Tenochtitlan, Nineveh—
has all but vanished. What birds there are don't sing.

Later, I learned I was right—that was beachgrass
(*Ammophila breviligulata*). As though knowing that helps.

THE DRIVEWAY

Sometimes my wife assigns me poems.
You have perhaps read some of them
if you have ever read me before.

Today she asked for a driveway poem,
possibly in an effort to call my attention
to the driveway's disrepair, its weedy
cracks, the holes that fill with rain.

Consequently, I am sitting with notebook
and a beer in a plastic chair in the drive
beneath the overhanging mulberry
and apple trees. Looking up, I can see
the blue jays' abandoned nest and a few
late mulberries hanging on. Otherwise,
the driveway's purple with them.

We talk sometimes of redoing the drive
with either brick or asphalt (cheaper)—
this stretch of concrete where balls
were kicked or dribbled, our feet
leaving its pocked surface for effortless
lay-ups, where the girls played four-square
and hopscotch, skated or rode bikes
down its slight decline through apple shadow.

It's here when small they threw the I Ching
with ball and jacks, sat chalking pictures
the rain washed away. It was here
the Mother-May-I game heard round the world
was played, and here one October
the good witch was saved from burning.

It was here someone was granted the serenity
to accept what could not be changed,
and here a Northwest Passage to the backyard
sought during the great blizzard of '78.
Upon this oil-stained surface we invented
fanfaronade, first danced the fandango,
debunked phallocentrism, witnessed
the birth of the blues, waved lonesome
farewells to those who would not return.

Notice our driveway's gentle curves,
its willingness to offer itself
as means, as end, as pubescent
proving ground, heresiarchic haven . . .
how naturally the snarled garden hose
finds a home here, how sturdily
the ladder rises from this firmness
toward the always disappointing gutters.

*   *   *

My wife will be back soon, pulling up
until she reaches my chair and empty
bottle, but I am finished anyway,
poetry having done what poetry
can sometimes do: fixing in the mind
what is fixed nowhere else.

POLITICAL POEM

I shouldn't have
but I did

not too often
but often enough

don't tell me
you didn't, wouldn't

MÖBIUS STRIP POEM

(with apologies to John Barth)

I'll never be as young again
as when I just sat down to write

Directions:
Cut out both lines, leaving a bit of blank space at the end of each;
Paste the second line upside down to the back of the first;
Twist the strip and paste the loose ends together.

NOT WITH A BANG OR A WHIMPER

. . . a breath and it is gone!
            —*Robert Browning*

For Paul Schaefer

Two weeks until Christmas. The Christ you believe in coming, you leaving. Perhaps your paths will cross. Neighbors ask what they can do. Friends from your church and the Amvets drop by, grandchildren are in and out, the priest come and gone. The kitchen table fills with food. Someone unearths a bottle of Johnny Walker Blue that won't outlive the day.

In the room where death is late arriving, I examine photos dim on the walls. The television, barely audible, is tuned to a channel featuring the Great American Songbook. Louis Armstrong rasps his way through something. Flowers, a ring of chairs. As for the hospital bed: what fits into such a thing?

Outside, I breathe the cold, watch cars pass on their way to or from wherever the unburdened go. A light snow falls. The flakes landing on my sleeve all look alike.

Annie Dillard says that anyone who rights a turtle overturned in the road has shown more compassion than God ever has. "Everyone," says Susan Sontag, "holds dual citizenship—in the kingdom of the well and in the kingdom of the sick." Or try Robert Creeley on for size: "No one is one / No one's alone." Has anyone the Bardo Thödol handy?

Sleet now where the sun should be. The sleet that never falls upward.

Now it's maybe Mel Tormé, now perhaps Ella. As each song begins, I turn to confirm who is singing what, turn back, and forget what I just read. Distractions: how, I guess, we manage in the midst of the dying, will manage after the death.

Ashes to ashes, we say; dust to dust. But there is no dust, no ashes. If only that were all this were.

Like dying itself, to watch someone die can be, among other things, tedious. Yet it is what we are already and always all about. Stiffening, drying out, running down. Misfiring, graying, shrinking, wrinkling. Cells misdividing, delusions of vigor. "Necrobiosis" is the word, programmed cell death. You name it, we've got it.

The phone rings and rings, calls coming in from the uninformed, the just informed. I watch grown men cry, lean down to kiss their father, make pointless adjustments to the blankets, open or shut the window a crack. Is it warm in here or isn't it? Do we want December in the room or not?

I wonder what sort of death I'm busy making down payments on. It is myself I grieve for.

I have been ignoring you, ignoring everyone save Johnny, overstaying my break in the kitchen. Back, I listen to your nurse daughter explain what the change in your breathing means, take your vitals, fiddle the morphine. I look at my wife watching her sister and see by her expression that she is suddenly ten years old again, and scared.

In *Heart of Glass*, the seer Hias remarks, "people make themselves at home as if they didn't want to leave this world, ever." Yet your son tells me that, since your wife died, you have been waiting eight years for this day. Is that why only you seem to be smiling?

Still, each breath is labored, a gurgling, a slow drowning. Eyes shut, mouth open, heartbeat fierce. We are assured that you are unaware, but this is small comfort. A test of faith for the Catholics present, those holding each other's hand. Making infrequent, irrelevant small talk. Leaving the room, returning—like Mel Tormé, whose turn has come round again, crooning, if you can believe it, "Body and Soul."

Someone asks if I would like a cup of coffee and, although vaguely ashamed to admit it, I say I would. The paper, also late arriving, tells of a couple who, drunk, crashed their car into a utility pole. Both died on the spot. I envy them. I envy the birds at the feeder.

I cannot stay focused, study again the pictures on the wall, sing silently along with Dean or Anita for a rhyme or two, move my undrunk coffee from floor to dresser, dresser to floor, offer my wife a sip, watch your children come and go, look out the window into the drizzle, the drear. I want all of us outside—the four brothers, three sisters, their wives, husbands, partners—where the ground is wet and cold, leaf-swept, muddy. I want everyone rolling in the mud, running and slipping and shouting in some game of freeze tag, breaking things, throwing something hard against the walls, through the windows, far away.

Or: I want to be alone in some elegant, dimly lit bar with a large glass of something expensive, reading things of interest only to those who can forget about death: budget deficits, Guggenheim retrospectives, shameless congressmen, pre-Christmas sales. Instead I toast a bagel and think hard about my choices: butter, jam, cream cheese.

Some version of each of us is disappearing before our eyes, some version of each other changing in each of us. Some version of ourselves. Your breathing too has altered again, grown shallower, each breath perhaps the last . . . but then another. The rest of us hold ours. "Breath," says Creeley, "breaks the heart when it stops."

I look at my wife, say "give me your hand. Take my hand." Now. I won't let go, and don't you. Despite this letting go, we won't.

Here in some third kingdom, we are all overturned turtles impossibly far from home. A home we will never return to all the way. As for the birds, they are nothing but a nuisance.

A DOVE

alit
in the almost leafless maple

I watched him
through my sickroom window
mortality heavy in my throat

it is not the war
makes me think such things
peace will not stop my dying

your dying

the leaves that hide the grass
came down one by one

the grass over his grave,
Whitman said, is himself

as for the leaves . . .
well, the leaves . . .

TWO ROBINS

Two upset robins
touch down noisily
at my feet
are gone almost
before they land
into the mulberry
and out, one
fleeing, one pursuing—
a territorial dispute
or foreplay, I
can't tell—out
of the apple
(how did they
get over there?)
onto the drive
eyeing one another
and then disappearing
around the corner
of the house.

The pursued returns
alights behind me
leaves for parts
unknown, the pursuer
arriving seconds later,
to sit cocking
his head, listening,
running a few
steps before stopping
to look again
here and there.

I returned to
what I'd been
doing. When I
looked again he
was off elsewhere
near the street
still running, stopping,
listening, as though
he couldn't believe
the other gone.

I understand him.
Often I too
want to be
sure of what
I can't believe.

CONNECT THE DOTS

I. PERIOD

The subject of the period brings Bob—known as "Bobert" to his friend Thom, who never reconciled himself to Bob's sudden desire to be called "Robert"—up short, stops him in his tracks. Moreover, thanks to his wife's present indisposition, Bob finds himself in a celibate period, which tends to make him a bit dotty. However, he will not expatiate, and should someone ask him what is wrong, he will reply curtly, "Nothing^{PERIOD}" Indeed, Bobert is occasionally given to the verbal punctuating of his sentences ("Are those new braces^{COMMA} Thom^{QUESTION MARK}") and found it fascinating that even in Arabic or Chinese one would encounter one's friend the period—something he discovered during periodic trips abroad during that full point in his life before radical surgery repunctuated him (see SEMICOLON), end stopped his former occupations. The books on his shelf (held up barely by two bent brackets), given over in whole or part to matters punctuative—from *The Harbrace College Handbook* to Lynne Truss—now sit unread above the easy chair where once Bobert, punctual as nature's menses, as the successive phases of the moon, would contemplate the comma, dote on the dash. Perhaps this silence is merely one of the two phrases composing the complete statement of his otherwise less than musical life; here, in any event, is his most recent word on the subject, a poem:

II. SEMICOLON

Bobert's semicolon was the result of radical surgery. It put a sort of stop to his life, though he knew there was more to come. Still, at the moment, he sat on his couch like a period atop a comma, his past and future linked vaguely in their mutual independence from his present state of mind. Say that Bobert was in a transitional phase; however, if his present was conjunctive vis-à-vis yesterday and tomorrow, it was equally liable to false connections; Bob was poised to mistake his nascent "survivor status" for the irretrievable loss of his erstwhile *joie de vivre*; let's say it was his introduction to new concerns that had little to do with what had come before, hence requiring a full stop while Bobert collected his thoughts and attempted to reassemble (like a model car— say, the '61 Corvette that has fallen from Bob's shaky shelf) the fragments of his belief in the consilience of what he thought he knew (that, for instance, William Whewell, who coined the term "consilience," as well as the term "scientist," was somehow responsible for Bobert's surgical abridgement, that these were somehow items closely related albeit in need of a strong conjunctive adverb—certainly, therefore, undoubtedly—or transitional phrase: as a result; granted that; as soon as).

III. BRACES

Bobert has no truck with braces, his life being, as it were, in parenthesis. Indeed, he lost whatever love he might once have had for such elegant enclosures (Thom says the world has had no need for braces since it ran out of eighteenth century) on the day at the doctor's when he had to brace himself for bad news. Leaving the office of "Dr. Hyphen," as Bobert referred to him, refusing to pronounce in toto the doctor's fancy, hyphenated surname, Bobert stopped for a bracer of Old Grand-Dad at a questionable bar from which he called Thom, to whom he could only exclaim excitedly, "my colon! My colon!" When Thom arrived, Bobert chose to overlook the fact that he was wearing braces (Thom being of generous girth although still embraceable, albeit not by Bobert) and, to make matters worse, some sort of skin bracer (Mennen or 'Lectric Shave). Bobert, the occlusion of whose teeth might have benefited from the application of braces—a fact to which Thom often reverted—had lately braced Thom for $10, but Thom let both topics rest that evening, choosing instead to observe that a brace of keypad keys is to this day devoted in part to the brace sinister and the brace dexter, for no reason Thom could see. Bobert hung fire, sipped his sour mash—courtesy of R.B. Hayden, distiller, of Hobbs Station, Kentucky—and idly ran a rope through a yardarm block left behind in the booth by some in-transit gob.

Was Bob's favorite band ? and the Mysterians? Well, wasn't he given to asking, "whatever happened to Rudy Martinez and the boys?" and "what were the two chords in '96 Tears'?" Was Bob given to asking questions of this sort? What does Thom say? When asked, Thom replies, "Of what sort?" Does Thom say that Bob is fond of questions Bob's answers to which send him (Bob) into fits of self-inflicted tee-hee?

> Bob: Did you know the supermarket is selling bread made by actual Trappist monks QUESTION MARK Do you know the wrapper boasts "no trans fats" QUESTION MARK
> Thom: So?
> Bob: Ah, but does it contain any Jumpin' Jehosephats QUESTION MARK

Have we another example?

> Bob: Don't you think the motto of the United States ought to be "Got milk" QUESTION MARK (Was Bob inspired to ask this because he happened at the time to be pouring two creamers into his breakfast coffee?)
> Thom: Why not, "Got apple pie?" (Did Thom then sit back to await the correct answer while dunking a doughnut into his café Americano?)
> Bob: Because that would be just stupid COMMA don't you see QUESTION MARK Isn't homogenized milk just like America's official motto *e pluribus unum* DITTO
> Thom: How so? Why isn't it like *Novus Ordo Seclorum*? For that matter, why isn't apple pie just like *Annuit Cœptis*? And, anyway, is *e pluribus unum* our official motto?
> Bob: *Our* motto YOU GUESSED IT
> Thom: Isn't it "In God We Trust"?
> Bob: Then shouldn't it be "In God We Trust QUESTION MARK"
> Thom: Bob, where do we come from? What are we? Where are we going?
> (Why was Thom pretending to be Paul Gauguin? Or was he?)

V. EXCLAMATION POINT

"Thom^{EXCLAMATION POINT}" Bob exclaims, "how can you reveal such things about me^{EXCLAMATION POINT} You know I am in a fragile state^{EXCLAMATION POINT} Why^{COMMA} I've lost part of my colon ^{EXCLAMATION POINT}" The look on Bob's phiz was an exclamatory "!" expressing both surprise and strong emotion . . . indeed, Thom had noticed that since Bobert's surgery, Bob was distractingly exclamatory, so much so that everything he said or did seemed an exaggeration! Before the removal of a comma's worth of colon, Bob, having been off and on an academic in spirit if not in fact, had not favored the use of exclamations on the theory that nothing excites or surprises a true intellectual!

When Thom was first apprised of Bob's notions vis-à-vis the sobriety if not the severity of intellectuals, the look that flitted across his ruddy visage was the familiar if slightly paradoxical "?!" Thom, you see, has always thought highly of the exclamation . . . indeed, to call a shovel a shovel,* Thom digs it because, if I might interject a perhaps sensitive detail, he finds it a kissing cousin to the ejaculation!

VI. COLON

---

* The more familiar phrase "to call a spade a spade" has been altered in deference to Thom's extreme sensitivity to racial connotations in the English language. To have employed "to call a spade a spade" would have provoked Thom to cry out, to give voice to a "sudden, vehement utterance" ("Exclamation," *Webster's New World Dictionary,* 2nd College Ed.). Our alteration, however, is not capricious but stands on a firm etymological foundation, viz.:

> *Brewer's Dictionary of Phrase and Fable* (1913) defines [to call a spade a spade] as "To be outspoken, blunt, even to the point of rudeness; to call things by their proper names without any 'beating around the bush.'" Its ultimate source is Plutarch's Apophthegmata Laconica (178B) which has την σκαφην σκαφην λεγοντας. σκαφη mean[ing] "basin, trough," but it was mis-translated as *ligo* "shovel" by Erasmus in his Apophthegmatum opus. Lucian *De Hist. Conscr.* (41) has τα συκα συκα, την σκαφην δε σκαφην ονομασων: "calling a fig a fig, and a trough a trough" (*Wikipedia: The Free Encyclopedia*).

NB: *Harper's* reported back in December, 2007, that a minimum of 310 edits to *Wikipedia* since June 2004 "have been traced back to the CIA," which I pass along *gratis* because you should know.

It is tempting to return at this point to Bobert's colon, which is still more or less in use. Or to introduce Cleveland/Montreal/Chicago/Anaheim/Los Angeles/Boston/Chicago pitcher Bartolo Colon (five wins, three losses so far this season, last time I looked), who is not, incidentally, from Cologne, although he may use cologne after a hot day on the mound. It is tempting at this point to make a bad joke about the use of cologne and being on the mound, or, in this case, the *mons* (a sometimes hirsute subject not to be confused with the Buddhist people of eastern Myanmar). But I will do neither. Neither will I stray into the arena of classical prosody, although that might be appropriate, wherein "colon" refers to "one of the members or sections of a rhythmical period, consisting of a sequence of from two to six feet united under a principal ictus or beat," according to Dictionary.com (which, today, perhaps not coincidentally, offers a link to the always arresting topic of colon cleansing). Nor has Bobert's colon much to do with colonial plantation owners (especially in Algeria) or the so-called monetary units of El Salvador or Costa Rica (Bartolo Colon is from the Dominican Republic, so his name should not be understood as the Spanish equivalent of Johnny Paycheck) (born Donald Eugene Lytle, Paycheck was imprisoned once for shooting a man and once for statuary rape; his death, from emphysema- and asthma-related complications, had nothing to do with his colon). None of which, alas, serves to properly introduce: Bob's colon.

VII. DASH

Bob needs to spice up his life—give it a pinch of pleasure, a touch of trouble, a dash of danger—"perhaps^{COMMA}" he thinks, "I should go into training for the Olympics^{DASH} say^{COMMA} the fifty^{HYPHEN}yard dash^{EXCLAMATION POINT}"—as he dashed to the door, only to have his hopes dashed because it was not the pizza man knocking but a brace of perambulating evangelists—one quite dashing—& in a fit of pique he dashes them both—in Morse Code, in a flurry of verbal dots and dashes—to counter what Bob considers the secret code of evangelism—but when Thom drops by, just as Bob is about to add a dash or three of Tabasco to his lately arrived cheese-and-pepperoni pizza, he—Thom—could only sputter "What?—What?!" to Bob's story, for as Bob relates how he dashed the petrified proselytizers' pamphlets to the pavement—"Is that personification?" Thom interjected; "No^{COMMA} you assonance-hole^{SEMICOLON} it's alliteration," snapped Bob parenthetically—his use of the verb "dashed"—in the transitive—sent Thom off on a reverie the burden of which was the cumbersome necessity of forming a dash when typing by double-striking the hyphen key, a flaw in keypad designers' thinking that could easily be remedied if one of the brace keys—say, the brace dexter—were devoted instead to the dash proper.

VIII. ELLIPSIS

Something is missing from Bobert's life ... something in addition to a stretch of his colon (see COLON; SEMICOLON) ... something, as we have seen, that now gives him pause and makes him brace himself for worse ... Thom, meanwhile, has taken a new job ... his friendship with Bob suffers ... as Thom meets obligations vocational and familial, Bob stews, feeling his days are numbered ... his woes numberless ... what words, he wonders, have been omitted from his new life's sentence ... and of the words remaining, had he dotted their *i*'s and crossed their *t*'s^{QUESTION MARK} ... do they match those that once completed the thought of him ... even if mismatched, ungrammatical, or "awk" (as his high-school teacher used to write beside any number of his efforts to express his often elliptical insights) ... Still, Bob finds the omission most inappropriate ... and penciled a Morse Code

"S" on the table so that he would not forget . . . but forget what?

-.. .- ... . | .. - | ..--.. |, he opined, and made a dash for another piece of pizza, pausing to clip a coupon taped to the lid of the box . . . cutting carefully along the dotted lines.

IX. FORWARD SLASH

It would be presumptuous to say anything regarding the forward slash.

X. HYPHEN

Bob has begun to st-st-stutter. A lover of the dash—his favorite fictional character is Aunt Em, his favorite writer of fiction Dashiel Hammett—Bob was once f-f-fond of the hyphen as well, but now it only presents pro-pro-pro-problems. Moreover, in his con-con-convalescent state, he has come to hate self-service gas stations, left-handed compliments related to his O-so-precarious health, Thom's fondness for Tex-Mex. Why this change of attitude toward the once-beloved hyphen is hard to explain. After all, when Bob's colon was partially excised, it was not as though a dash had been inserted between the remaining sections—a colon with a gap being of precious little utility—but conjoined, hyphenated, as it were, by his surgeon, or so muses Bob when contemplating what he hopes will prove a once-in-a-lifetime medical adventure. As for the excised one and five-eighths inches, it was doubtless dashed into a pail of soon-to-be-discarded medical waste, the oft-regretted loss of which has rendered Bob less self-possessed, more self-absorbed, and—oddly—anti-hyphen.

XI. APOSTROPHE[*]

Since his surgery, Bob's been experiencing contractions of the bowels, which have made him—you guessed it—irritable. He's also developed the conviction that Thom is repeating everything he says. "He says," reveals Thom, "that he can't believe I would 'steal [his] words' (to say nothing of his 'thunder') and thereby 'betray him.'" Moreover, Thom reports that Bob's lost his former interest in baseball, never speaking as once he did about "Bartolo Colon or 'Sudden' Sam McDowell." As for rock 'n' roll, weeks pass with no questions regarding ? and the Mysterians . . . it's sad," concludes Thom. "Bob's even stopped punctuating his sentences: no more 'I don[APOSTROPHE]t believe it,' no sirree! Our friendship, which had recapitulated the history of contractions," opines Thom, "has now shifted into reverse.[**] When first we met, it was 'do not,' then 'do nt,' then 'don't'— well, really, 'don[APOSTROPHE]t'—which as you can clearly see signaled a growth in intimacy, casualness, and comfort—but now (I guess it's those post-traumatic-stress contractions) Bobert's returned to addressing me with the formality of a business letter." Thom slashes at the ground with a comma-shaped stick before adding, "Bob's even given up on the possessive case . . . I'm at 6's and 7's . . . and y'all can quote me on that."

XII. COMMA

Despite Bobert's (presently waning) punctuphilia, to talk about the comma always gave him pause—for it is indeed the Coca Cola of points, the rest stop that refreshes on the

---

[*] The author is well aware that apostrophes and single quotation marks serve different punctuative purposes and both apologizes for muddily mingling them here and thanks all those who have pointed this error out to him. He does, however, maintain that visually they are identical, as any fool can see.

[**] Alas, matters of grammar and usage fall outside the parameters of this story.

way to one's final destination, although to stop is only to begin again, often as not, as this very sentence demonstrates, like it or not. It—the comma—is a place to linger, to savor the trip so far, while the promise of revelation blossoms and the frustration of confusion may yet be resolved. It is a small clarification of the journey, like the maps outside the turnpike restrooms that tell us "You Are Here," and we see that exit fifteen is in fact not our exit, as we thought, just as the comma's absence is in itself a clarification: that it is not that *all* patients both lose part of their colons and experience bowel contractions ("all patients, who lose part of their colons, experience bowel contractions") but only those who find themselves in a semicolonic state who find themselves with griped guts ("all patients who lose part of their colons experience bowel contractions"). (If indeed they do.)

On the other hand, one reads that *vibrio cholerae* is "a comma-shaped bacterium," infesting the intestines and inducing both vomiting and what one medical text terms "massive diarrhoea" on its way through one's bowels, through eventually large intestine to colon (or, in Bob's case, should he ever succumb, to semicolon) to rectum in explosive, "rice water" excretions: hardly a pause calculated to refresh. Nevertheless, Bobert could use a few commas to splice his life together, or perhaps the removal of same to fuse the fragments left from too much thinking about Bartolo Colon, the period, and Thom's braces.

XIII. SLASH

Increasingly, Bob is given to cutting remarks that have sliced off a few of Thom's emotional pockets and buttons, rough and sweeping invective, Errol Flynn swordplay wedded to W.C. Fields barbs that serve, oddly, both to divide and to unite the two friends: Bob/Thom. Thom remains sanguine, feeling that if the two were once a rhymed couplet, they are now that same couplet but embedded in a paragraph of prose. Nevertheless, he cannot help feeling that the value of their relationship has been drastically reduced.

What do you think, Bob?

1) Is Thom correct? Yes/No (circle one)

2) Is this an either/or situation? Yes/No (circle one)

3) Is yours an on-again/off-again relationship? Yes/No (circle one)

4) Are you clearing mental space for arable purposes? Yes/No (circle one)

5) Is Thom now a friend and/or enemy? (circle 5/16 of one choice and 1/16 of the other)

6) Are you attempting to slit the outer fabric of your personality to reveal your true colors? Yes/No (circle one)

7) In the space below, please reveal your inner-most thoughts and feelings as of 6/8/18:

_____

_____

_____

_____

_____

_____

_____

When Thom and Bob were single, they often double-dated. Thom, attempting to effect a rapprochement, recalls an evening with Deb and Dottie at Mr. Larry's Beef and Tails, causing Bob to sneer, "May I quote you? Can you give me a quote on what I should bid for 'your' words from my mouth?"

Thom, who had once imagined that the story of their friendship would eventually be so eventful and rich, hence lengthy, that, if ever written down and titled, its title would be italicized, now fears he is rather nearing the end of a short story. Tears threaten Thom's malar regions ("malar": "relating to the cheek"). Still, Thom "presses on," saying he finds Bob's remarks "amusing," arcing two fingers of each hand through a brief space of air to indicate sarcasm.

"You find my remarks <small>QUOTATION MARK</small>amusing<small>QUOTATION MARK QUESTION MARK</small>

"'You find my remarks "amusing"?'"Thom parrots, although the remark is not especially quotable.

"I find *you* 'amusing.'" (Four fingers inscribing Bob's own sarcasm in Thom's face.)

"Quotha!" smiles Thom, although whether he is expressing surprise or contempt is difficult to say. One supposes the former. Certainly it is surprise that registers on Bob's mug: "!"

"'!' indeed," says Thom, shaking his "noggin" sadly.

XV. BRACKETS

That Thom and Bob find braces a racket has been established (see BRACES), but both, despite their recent differences, admire the serviceable bracket, its several scholarly uses. True, its work is sporadic, its income therefore placing it in a lower-income bracket, yet it is most respectable work; like the secretary of a busy businessman, the bracket (both dexter and sinister) is indispensable if often intrusive. Just so Bob's wife (his current wife, wife #4, is here meant), whose frolicsome forays into Bob's withdrawn life were like insertions and clarifications into his parenthetical days and often merely quoted emotions [sic], which (i.e., those "frolicsome forays") Bob often recited to himself when Thom was unavailable.

But to bracket such details and return to Thom's remark about "find[ing] [his, i.e., Thom's] remarks 'amusing'"—why has Bob, his semicolon and his attendant emotional ejaculations notwithstanding, hung up his *joie de vivre* like a flower basket from a front-porch bracket? Clearly, Bob is in need of support here in the bracket between his life's explosions: after all, is ours not a right-angle relationship with God, and is it not true that we read in 1 John 4:20 (see also Mark 12:31), "He that loveth not his brother whom he hath seen, how can he love God whom he hath not seen?" Bob's brackish response: "Thom is not my ^{QUOTE} brother^{CLOSE QUOTE PERIOD}"

XVI. PARENTHESES

Although he sees egress both above and beneath him, Bob feels trapped within some enclosure that has separated him from the main idea of his life. (He feels, he says, like David Jones [not to be confused with Davy Jones of the Monkees].) His parenternal life is fine if sometimes paresthetic (it does not take "guts" to live it); indeed, his intestinal life is likewise fine (although it does take guts to live *it*). Nonetheless, Bob— with or without Thom and wife #4 by his side (and whether he loses himself in contemplation of Bartolo Colon, ? and the Mysterians, or the stylistic difference between "and" and "&")—feels paresis coming on and parenthesizes this fear whenever it up-wells. In short: (Bob + semicolon) + Thom

(+ or − wife #4) ≠ happiness. May the Paraclete (in Middle English, *Paraclit*, which makes Thom blush) both advocate for and comfort Bob.

& until a new mark of punctuation is invented, here we must leave him.

LEAF SQUIRREL

a leaf
a breeze
I al-

most braked

THE MAN AT THE DUMP

Emerging from a shack inside
a chain-link fence festooned
with hubcaps and old license plates,
the man at the dump eyed me
with evident distaste. He had a dog,
an unchained squittering of snarls.
His hair, like mine, was long and tangled.
Indeed he looked a lot like me—filthy work
shirt, filthier jeans, filthiest boots—
though this did not incline him
to be receptive to my pathetic load
of apparently substandard trash,
though receive it he must,
directing me with a pointed "over there"
to a moldering mound of who-
knows-what where I might deposit
my miserable trunk of junk.

"Earth laughs in flowers," said
Emerson. If so, there is no laughter here
beneath the hovering birds of stink,
the toxic plumes of decay, rubbish
fires vomiting smut, monstrous engines
of crush and shove and bury.
On the other hand, the Buddha
tells us that "a sweet-smelling lotus
blooms upon a heap of filth."
Perhaps. For all that, "pulchritudinous"
is not a word often spoken here.

On my way out, this guardian of garbage
leans into the car to growl at me

for leaving my broken offerings
upon the wrong smoldering tumulus.
"Couldn't put it where I told you,"
he snarls. Does he want it moved?
He does not. We are both on the thin
edge of civility, but because "restraint
in all things is good," I roll up
the window and drive slowly away,
thinking how some day someone
will enjoy him with a sharp knife.

Still, what do I know about this monk
of the dump with his dog-pound Cerberus,
his muddy tattoo and abused hands,
who owns what no one else wants,
who knows that into every life
a little rust must fall. Maybe he knows
he is where he belongs, matter learning
to love matter, even, or especially,
the matter that to others does not matter.
Where decay frolics and wastes away,
he knows that we are ashes, that we are dust,
but also knows, perhaps, perhaps,
that here, beyond the fetor and disgust,
beyond the all that time consumes
the spotless, fragrant lotus blooms.

RAINOUTS

1.

Ball games, mostly, the joy
of release, even from one's
pleasures, the opening of time . . .

sit awhile, have another beer,
nothing needs doing, the possibility
of defeat for now delayed

2.

Let it be raining, Lord,
when I die, that we
might sit awhile, and share

a drink, some small talk,
watching the world grow wet,
all final decisions happily deferred

NOTES

Sudden Sam ("Why I Like Baseball") is Samuel Edward Thomas McDowell, who pitched for Cleveland from 1961 – 1971 before moving on to the Giants, Yankees, and Pirates.

U.S. Camera ("Posing") was a popular magazine when my father was young and getting interested in photography. Although I am sure this played no part in his interest, the magazine was also one of the few periodicals where at the time one might encounter photos of nude women.

After reading "A Mary Haggadot," a friend wrote to inform me that I didn't know my Bible very well. Some time later, I received in the mail from Mitch Finley a copy of his book *Surprising Mary: Meditations and Prayers on the Mother of Jesus.* A note directed my attention to certain pages, where I found one of my poems quoted as an example of "what the Assumption of Mary is about," so I wrote to my friend to let him know that I was perhaps a poor Protestant but apparently a hell of a Catholic.

Alopecia areata, which occasioned the poem of the same name, is a hair-loss condition with a diverse etiology and without a cure.

The final line of "The Lecture on Dust" is taken from Daniel Thompson's *Even the Broken Letters of the Heart Spell Earth.*

"Plastic Fantastic Lovers" is the slightly altered title of a 1967 song by the Jefferson Airplane.

For my younger readers: watches once had to be wound by hand ("Winding My Watch") and, yes, it was exhausting.

The line in "Interview with a Suicide" about the moonlight going crazy is doubtless a memory-mangled appropriation of a line from Jonathan Edwards' song "Margaret." His line is better, so he shouldn't mind.

The nine poems comprising "Shoshaku Jushaku" were written under the influence of Shunryu Suzuki's *Zen Mind, Beginner's Mind* (from which the quotations that open each section come) . . . and, of course, that of the woman they pursue. Stanza three of part five ends with lines lifted from three songs: Alejandro Escovedo's "Broken Bottle," Jimmie Rodgers' "Dreaming with Tears in My Eyes," and Bob Dylan's "Don't Think Twice." The first stanza of part six ends with and modifies a remark once made by Gary Snyder, who (if I recollect correctly) confessed to having himself borrowed the observation from a friend.

"Calling Time" was inspired by a photograph in Terry Pluto and Tony Kubek's *Sixty-One: The Team, the Record, the Men*; in the photograph—a publicity shot—Rollie Sheldon and manager Ralph Houk pretend to listen to and admire the watch Rollie has been awarded as the most promising rookie at spring training.

The beginning of "One Tuesday" improvises upon the opening lines of the *Tao Te Ching* as rendered by Stephen Mitchell. Other appropriations and allusions here are too obvious to note.

"Shekinah," among its meanings, is defined by Rebbe Mordechai Gafni as "the feminine divine."

"Satyagraha" ("Ararat from the Flood") is Gandhi's term for "living in truth." In the same poem, "Moulana Rumi" is a reference to the Persian poet, sometimes known as "our master Rumi." "Sohbet" is meant in the sense of "mystical conversation" (definition courtesy of Coleman Barks). The final line reworks the final line of Rilke's "Archaic Torso of Apollo."

"(Un)Sexy Mearns," I must make clear, was a challenge taken up in a fit of *joie de vivre* after reading about the poet Hughes Mearns. It is not autobiographical, as my wife fears readers will conclude. A "mearns" is rather a poem written in imitation of Mearns's "Antigonish." As defined by that scholar of forgotten poetry Martin Gardner, a mearns is "a quatrain about something or someone not there."

The italicized parts of "I Thought We'd Never Get Over That First Album" are taken from the lyrics of the MC5's album, *Kick Out the Jams* (1969).

"The Three Great Ideas of Yacouba Sawadogo" is based closely on an article by Mark Hertsgaard in *The Nation*, 7 December 2009.

Ko Un ("Two for Ko Un") is South Korea's preeminent poet and a frequent Nobel Prize nominee.

Phil Ochs, mentioned in "Snapshots of China," was a folksinger/songwriter and activist who, in the early Sixties, gave Bob Dylan a run for his money. Ochs's best-known songs are probably "There But for Fortune" and "I Ain't Marchin' Any More." He preferred calling himself a "topical singer."

"Snapshots of China" was written during a few weeks spent traveling at the invitation of Beijing's *Guangming Daily* as part of a small group of Kent State University professors. Pratim is a Professor of management; Norm was at the time a professor of accounting. Mr. He Nong, who accompanied us throughout the visit, was an editor with the newspaper and acquired the nickname "Renaud" while covering Europe from his base in Paris. Molly: you somehow didn't find your way into any of these poems, but I haven't forgotten how the two of us drank our way across China.

The apologies to John Barth ("Möbius Strip") acknowledge his "Frame-Tale" in *Lost in the Funhouse*. This note itself is a nod to either the "the anxiety of influence" or the sincerest form of flattery.

INDEX OF TITLES AND FIRST LINES

A poet, professor, and scholar, BROOKE HORVATH grew up in Elyria, Ohio. He is the author of three previous books of poetry, *In a Neighborhood of Dying Light*, *Consolation at Ground Zero*, and *The Lecture on Dust*, as well as a book of criticism, *Understanding Nelson Algren*. He co-edited, with Dan Simon, Algren's *Entrapment and Other Uncollected Writings*, also published by Seven Stories Press. Horvath is Emeritus Professor of English at Kent State University and splits his time between Kent, Ohio, and Fredonia, New York.